LOOKING GOOD
GOOD
ILLUSIONS OF BEAUTY

D1463025

About the author:

Dr. Ann Clark is president of Ann Clark Associates, Inc., a national employee assistance firm. A widely published author, Dr. Clark's popular booklet, *Alone, But Not Lonely*, published by Hazelden Educational Materials, was featured by Associated Press in newspapers across the country. Her research on "Women, Alcohol, and the Workplace," a two-part series, and "Supervisory Referrals: The Untapped Resource" were published by the Almacan. *Surrender to Win* and *Single Parent Families* (published by Hazelden) are other works authored by Dr. Clark. On the popular "Donahue," she addressed "right to treatment" issues, and her articles have appeared in *Glamour* as well as in newspapers and professional magazines.

An executive as well as an active member of many professional associations, Dr. Clark received her doctorate from the University of Wisconsin and completed post-doctoral research on Alcoholism and Sexuality at the University of New Mexico. She is one of the original Certified Employee Assistance Professionals in the country.

LOOKING GOOD

ILLUSION & REALITY

IMAGES OF SOBER WOMEN

ANN D. CLARK, Ph.D.

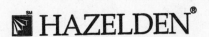

HAZELDEN

First published August 1990.

ISBN: 0-89486-695-8
Library of Congress Catalog Card Number: 90-81519

Printed in the United States of America.

Editor's note:
   Hazelden Educational Materials offers a variety of information on chemical dependency and related areas. Our publi-
cations do not necessarily represent Hazelden or its programs,
nor do they officially speak for any Twelve Step organization.
   The stories in this book are about real people; all names are
used with permission.

Contents

Acknowledgments — Gratitude List

A technique I learned early in Twelve Step meetings was making a gratitude list. What a useful tool, and where would it be more relevant than here?

Without the fellowship, I could not have written this book. I would not be living this life. The women and men of the program are the air that I breathe, my lifeblood, and my hope for the future. My heartfelt thanks to those who have gone before me and who've led me along this path of recovery.

To my daughters, Deanna and Tandice, I owe the greatest debt. Their encouragement, support, love, and friendship — no matter what — has been constant and unconditional. It is to them and my son-in-law Randy, equally supportive and loving, that I dedicate this book. We are today, as the Big Book says, "the family after."

And it is the recovering women, my dearest friends as well as strangers in the fellowship, that deserve the credit for this book. Special thanks to my best friend Alice, who has given me gifts beyond words; to Eadie, for her never-ending enthusiasm; to Patt, whose spiritual path shows me the way; to Annalee, my first mentor; and to Trudy, my first "sponsee." Thank you to the many women and men who have given so generously of their love and encouragement, their time and energy, to carry the message of sobriety to me and to you. It is to these women and men that this book belongs.

Finally, my thanks to Wendy Haskett for her tireless work in interviewing, recording, and transcribing. Her boundless energy for typing, retyping, and editing this manuscript, and her "normie" reactions to my words are all a part of this effort. And I must acknowledge my first editor at Hazelden, Brian Lynch, who envisioned this project.

To alcoholic and addicted women and men everywhere, to all those in recovery, my thanks to you, and my prayers.

ANN D. CLARK, PH.D.

Introduction —
"Looking Good"

> *My boss at the airlines said, "You can't be an alcoholic. You were never drunk on a flight. And you always look terrific."*
>
> — MARILYN, thirty-eight
> A former flight attendant

> *"Cindy, you're not an alcoholic!" my doctor said when I told him that I thought that, maybe, I was. "You're a fantastic woman!" He was smiling at me. I left his office feeling desperate.*
>
> — CINDY, forty-one
> A nursing supervisor

A lot of people would also have described me, in my drinking days, as "a fantastic woman," at least in the earlier years. My low self-esteem, my feelings of not being good enough were invisible.

If you and I were to meet today you might notice, gleaming on a chain around my neck, something that is visible. It's the coin-shaped gold token that I gave myself when I'd been sober for five years. It's a symbol for me. A symbol of my own sense of dignity and growing self-worth. It also reminds me that it wasn't until I entered recovery that I began to realize that "looking good" is an inside job.

Like so many alcoholics and addicts, I felt so worthless inside that my outside, and everything connected to me, *had* to look good. If it didn't then, maybe, someone might guess my secret. . . .

My whole family was concerned with appearances. I remember when my mother was dying she said, "Wear navy blue, Dear. It goes with everything." I was thirteen years old,

1

and this poor woman, ravaged by addiction, was so concerned with how I looked — not how I felt — that she was still worrying about my clothes when she was close to death.

Years later, when my addiction had progressed to the point where I was waking up every morning feeling that something bad was going to happen that day (because bad things happened to me so often by then) I was still an achiever. I was still standing behind lecture podiums depressed in beautiful clothes. I was desperate, despairing, and in unbelievable pain. My body was so addicted I even took a can of beer into the shower with me. But I looked good!

Recovery has been a joyous, adventurous, often painful process of self-examination and change. The coin around my neck is *also* a symbol to me of all the "slippery places" — the challenges to sobriety — I've successfully passed through. Many of these challenges have happened to me simply because I was a woman.

Simply because I was a woman?

But alcoholism is a disease. Surely it's the same disease whether you are a man or a woman?

It certainly is.

Both men and women in recovery are working through the same painful process of making lifestyle and personality changes in order to learn how to live comfortably as sober people. Men and women share many of the same challenges.

But not all of them.

This book is about the "slippery" places that are unique to us as women. It's about discovering creative ways to survive them, without drinking or using or being self-destructive in more subtle ways. You'll find most of the suggestions threaded through the stories of real women — women who have achieved success in sobriety. This is also a "blended" book. I've blended my own story, which is true, with that of a fictional woman, a young journalist named Terry.

Terry is a composite of several recovering women I know. In these stories I've shared a great many intimate details to illustrate to you what has worked for us. (Believe it or not, many of the things that happened to us in new sobriety were fun!) And all of the recovering women who shared their experiences for these pages did so because they hoped they could make sobriety just a little easier for someone else.

Recovery isn't easy. It isn't quick. But it's *do-able.*

CHAPTER ONE

My Name Is Ann, And I'm a Recovering Alcoholic

Picture the laundry room of a trailer park in Arizona. It's the middle of an August morning and the Formica countertop, a lurid acid yellow, feels warm to the touch.

I'm standing on an upturned tub, a freckled nine-year-old with braids, folding my family's laundry. The voices of two women who have just left the room drift in through the open window. They are talking about me.

"Poor little thing. She shouldn't have to do all that. . . ."

"A shame. . . ."

"The mother drinks. . . ."

"And the fights! You can hear them all over the . . ."

Anger clenches inside me.

I want to run after them, tell them that I'm doing the laundry because I *want* to. I offered to do it. In my family, I'm a big help. My family is fine!

I feel very hostile toward those women.

I hoist the laundry basket on my hip and walk slowly back toward our trailer. I don't hear the gravel crunching under my shoes. I don't notice the dusty cactus growing beside the path. My mind is too busy, bending reality so that my world looks good. *Now* the women in the laundry room are rescripted. Now, I imagine them saying, "Isn't that little girl amazing? Her mother's an invalid, poor woman. They moved here from Kentucky because of her asthma. And the father's real busy setting up a new law practice in town. How that family would have managed without Ann, I don't know. She's a wonderful cook, as well as looking after her baby brothers. Her daddy must be so proud of her. . . ."

The sound of my father's voice coming from inside the trailer — a voice roaring in anger — jerks me out of my reverie.

He's come home for lunch.

I put down the basket. Is he angry with me? At my mother? At one of my brothers?

"This place looks like a pigsty!" my father shouts as, cautiously, I open the door. "And you call *that* a lunch?" His clenched fist slams down on the kitchen counter. A plate of Velveeta cheese on white bread sandwiches rattles. A bottle of milk topples sideways, sending a stream of milk onto the floor.

My mother, lying on the sofa, is crying softly. My baby brother is crying loudly. My four-year-old brother is nowhere in sight.

"Daddy — I'll make you lunch! I'll do it," I say. I stick a bit of Velveeta sandwich into the baby's mouth to quiet him. I grab a dishcloth and begin to wipe up the milk.

I am a good little girl, and an angry little girl. . . .

* * *

My name is Ann, and I'm a recovering alcoholic. My life today is a fabulous one. I have days when I don't think it could get any better. But it wasn't always so. My earliest memories are of confusion, fear, striving, and anger.

My mother was often kind and sweet to me, but she was too weak to defend me or my younger brothers from my father's rages. He beat us brutally, and he raged at her.

She was an iatrogenic addict — addicted to drugs carelessly prescribed by physicians. As the eldest of her three children, the only daughter, it was my job to give her the daily injections of Demerol prescribed for her asthma. Demerol is a synthetic morphine. From the age of nine or ten, I would run down to the local pharmacy for a refill, and they would calmly hand it over to me.

My father was handsome, intelligent, alcoholic, and totally unpredictable. My grandparents were alcoholics, too, and so were all the relatives I can remember. Of course, I didn't have a label for them then. They were my family. In spite of the pain and chaos, I loved them.

On that hot August morning in the Arizona trailer park, I used my thoughts to alter the reality of a life I hated and couldn't understand. At nine, it was my way of coping.

A few years later, I began using alcohol to alter my reality, and then prescription drugs starting at eighteen when a doctor prescribed Valium because I told him I was having anxiety attacks. Prescriptions were a nuisance to get, so I moved on to street "speed" next, then cocaine as well, working up to larger and larger amounts and lacing the mixture with "crystal." But alcohol was always my drug of "choice." The pain and hopelessness generated by this way of life eventually drove me to attempt suicide twice.

Do you remember the story of Pinocchio — the boy puppet whose nose grew longer whenever he told a lie? When I was struggling through early sobriety (and when I say struggling I mean to the point that my mind was so confused I had trouble deciding if I should brush my teeth), a friend gave me a Pinocchio doll.

"Prop him up on your dresser," she said, giving me a hug. "He's a reminder to be honest."

Telling the truth can be very hard for us when we are recovering from an addiction — partly because we often don't know what *is* real, what is true, from one moment to the next. Yet honesty is vital to recovery. People who are honest with themselves will often say that fear dominated their first year of recovery.

That first year I was going to AA meetings, I sat at the back of the room, and I didn't say a word. To anyone.
— CONNIE, seventy-two

Almost everything scared me. It was like being up to my knees in alligators.
— GAIL, thirty-six

* * *

In very early sobriety, even a first day can be scary. It can be a slippery place for us.

* * *

The anxiety that Terry has been feeling all day heightens as she sits down at the restaurant table across from Jeff. Of course I'm nervous, she thinks. It's my first date since my divorce. My first date in eighteen months of sobriety. Before, I would have boosted my courage by drinking all the time I was getting dressed. . . .

A cheerful female voice breaks into her thoughts. "Hi, my name is Chelsea, and I'll be your waitress for tonight. Can I get you something to drink?"

Jeff is smiling. In the glow from the red-fringed table lamp his face looks tanned and handsome. He doesn't seem anxious. Of course not, why should he be? He has no idea that she's a recovering alcoholic. This evening isn't a big deal for him.

"How about some champagne?" he suggests. "To celebrate."

Champagne! Such an elegant drink. The drink of weddings and anniversaries. She would love some champagne.

"No, thank you," she hears her voice saying. "That's a lovely thought, Jeff. But I'd like Perrier."

"You don't drink?"

Now he'll think she's dull. What should she tell him? How much should she tell him?

"I had some health problems," she says cautiously. "So I quit drinking."

"Well, gosh, I really admire that."

He is, Terry realizes, as dinner progresses, a nice guy. He seems genuinely interested in her work as a feature writer in the business section of the city's largest newspaper. He's thirty-three, the owner of his own printing business. Like her he's newly divorced.

"I've always liked kids," he says, sipping at a glass of chardonnay. He's sipping slowly, Terry notices. No closet alcoholic here. "I was really sorry that my ex-wife and I didn't have any kids."

Terry's mind skips instantly to a fantasy scenario. She's in the park on a summer Sunday with her children, five-year-old Cody, and seven-year-old Beth. Jeff, now her husband, is playing Frisbee with Cody and a golden retriever puppy. She and Beth are watching, sitting on a blanket, laughing. Jeff strides suddenly across the grass toward them. He bends to kiss her. . . .

Across the table the real Jeff is speaking to her.

"What. . . ? I'm sorry?"

"I said there's live music over in the bar. A local band called Pineapple Nights. Okay with you?"

Not really, she thinks, as Jeff, his hand firmly under her elbow, steers her into the clatter and jangle of the bar. The Pineapple Nights are six young men in Hawaiian shirts, playing something that sounds like calypso music. Chelsea, the friendly blond waitress, passes them, her long tanned legs flashing beneath her thigh-high, wraparound skirt.

By comparison to Chelsea, Terry feels plain and faded. A small inner voice of logic struggles to remind her that she's only thirty-one. Her dark hair is naturally curly. Strangers in places like the supermarket often comment on what a pretty face she has. She's anything but faded! But tonight she feels as if she is.

One of the things she'd liked about drinking was that it always made her feel attractive.

Sexy.

Confident.

Carefree.

"Sit here," *Jeff murmurs, maneuvering her into a corner seat.
"I'll get something from the bar. Coffee for you?"*
"Yes. Thanks."

*He is nice. And he'll probably never want to see her again.
Ben, her husband of nine years, didn't want to see her again. Ben
said she'd changed too much since she quit drinking. He'd complained that she was always out at meetings. He'd complained that
when she was home she was too quiet, too wrapped up in her own
thoughts, no fun. . . .*

*Jeff is weaving his way toward her, holding two coffee cups. He
looks pleased with himself. As he slides a cup in front of her, a strong
smell of whiskey rises from it.*

"Irish coffee," *he says.* "The bartender recommended it. That
won't hurt you, surely?"

*The Irish coffee didn't get a chance to hurt Terry. She eased her
feeling of panic by dashing off to the ladies room, and calling her
sponsor from a pay phone, while people jostled past her in the narrow
corridor, and the sounds of Pineapple Nights filtered faintly from
the bar.*

* * *

I could have been Terry. I *have* been Terry. In spite of all
the wonderful things I now have in my life — two beautiful
daughters, my own company, a circle of friends who cheer me
on — I still find my old feelings of not being good enough keep
creeping back. Self-esteem is something I have to work on
every day.

Life in sobriety does keep getting better and better. It can't
happen to us overnight though. Recovery takes time, and in
new sobriety most of us are running scared. ("As scared as if
I'd been knee-high in alligators," I heard one woman say at a
meeting.) Of course we're frightened. Who wouldn't be?
We're so vulnerable at this stage. We're like someone who has
walked through life with a cardboard cutout of herself held up
in front. It wasn't really *us* — but we hoped people would
think it was! Now all our protective shields are gone!

Slippery places are scary. They are the places where we can get so discouraged, we feel like giving up and drinking or using again.

Dating is definitely a slippery place. Men are a major influence in our lives, yet many of us in early sobriety feel, as Terry did, that without the confidence alcohol gave us we've lost most of our ability to be charming, or witty, or sexy. Many of us are afraid we might have lost our attractiveness. (This also works both ways. A dull, boring date can seem a lot more attractive to you when you're drinking.)

What are some of the other challenges we are likely to come up against? Here's a glimpse of the most common ones.

Physical Recovery

> *My whole body seemed to rebel. I was feeling tired one minute and hyper the next. I had aches and pains I'd never felt before, and my hands seemed to want to fly off the ends of my wrists. I thought,* I'm falling apart! Is this sobriety? I can't stand feeling this way!
> — SARAH, thirty-one
> A word processor, now
> recovering from cocaine
> abuse and anorexia for
> three years

* * *

It can be depressing to discover that, in *early* sobriety, you seem to be functioning far less efficiently than you did when you were drinking.

The stress of physical recovery is very complex in women. It's complicated by the delicately balanced female hormonal system, so easily upset. It can take a long time — varying with each individual — for our body to get back to a natural rhythm. So, at least in the beginning,

Feeling Physically Unwell Is a Very Slippery Place for Us

So, too, for nearly all women and many men, is the way we grew up.

Childhood and Family Recovery

I was seven when my grandfather started coming to my bedroom and sexually abusing me. He came every night. I tried to tell my grandmother, but she wouldn't listen to me. I began sleepwalking. Biting my nails. Wetting my pants. And the whole family pretended that nothing was wrong. That was the way my family dealt with things.

— LEAH, thirty-eight
A nurse in an intensive
care unit

I was the good girl in the family, a mother to my younger brother and sister from the age of eight. My father was gone a lot. My mother was a daily drinker. I cleaned vomit off her feet. I dealt with the police when they came to the door, after the neighbors had called them. "My dad will be home tomorrow," I'd tell them. "We're okay. I'll take care of everything."

— MARY, forty-two
A mental health counselor

* * *

Many of us never really dealt with the pain of dysfunctional family relationships. Nor with the emotional and behavioral consequences. We are more likely than men to have been overburdened with domestic responsibilities as children. A very high percentage of us were victims of sexual abuse.

Even a family that hasn't the dramatic problems Mary's and Leah's had — a family that, like the one Terry grew up in, looks white-picket-fence-perfect to outsiders — can be highly destructive to those who live inside it.

Carrying Unresolved Anger from Bad Family Relationships Is a Very Slippery Place for Us

Then there are

Society's Expectations

The hand that rocks the cradle mustn't shake.
— From the Book *The Invisible Alcoholics* by Marian Sandmaier

✳ ✳ ✳

Many people still think in stereotypes — they think of an alcoholic woman as a bag lady with wine in her shopping cart. Or, if she hasn't gone down quite that far yet, then she's haggard, bleary-eyed, and habitually stumbles around in a chenille bathrobe at ten in the morning.

✳ ✳ ✳

My husband and family just wouldn't believe I was an alcoholic. I'd been mixing Valium and alcohol for ten years. I was desperate and wanted to check into a hospital. They kept telling me I just needed to exercise more self-control. My husband said My God, Geri, If you went into one of those treatment centers, what would people think?
— GERI, twenty-nine

✳ ✳ ✳

Now divorced and two years into recovery from alcohol and prescription drug abuse, Geri is in law school.

✳ ✳ ✳

> *I remember my boss at one airline saying, "You don't look like an alcoholic. You were never drunk on a flight."*
> — MARILYN D., thirty-eight
> A former flight attendant

✳ ✳ ✳

The *reality*, borne out by numerous studies, is that the majority of alcoholic women today have homes, jobs, and families when they hit bottom.

Dealing with the past — recognizing that society often expected too much of us — is an important step in recovery.

One of the slipperiest places of all is concern about our

Relationships

> *I got married so I wouldn't have to get sober.*
> — STEPHANIE, twenty-eight
> A receptionist, in recovery
> from addiction to alcohol
> and crystal

> *A roll in the hay is not a relationship.*
> — "BOSTON" HELEN, eighty-two
> More than twenty-five
> years sober

> *When I got sober I looked at my husband of thirty years, and I didn't even like him.*
> — CONNIE, seventy-two
> A former radio actress, in
> recovery for ten years

✳ ✳ ✳

The word *relationship*, of course, applies to everyone we are close to. Our friends. Our family. Our co-workers. But, from flirtation to marriage, the relationship most of us constantly focus on is the male/female one. And most of us have had a lot of problems with that one.

Our relationships with men, established while we were abusing and before we've resolved our childhood and family conflicts, is apt to be based on poor choices. Considering the family turmoil most of us came from, we could hardly be expected to make healthy ones!

Sharon, who is now twenty-six and using a small inheritance to get through college, is bright and attractive. Until she got into a recovery program, though, she always felt she was worthless. "I felt ugly — dirty inside," she says. She had a rootless childhood, rattling around from state to state with a mother who went from man to man, several of whom sexually abused Sharon.

By age nineteen, she was living with a man who hit her, kicked her, told her she was stupid, and who had another girlfriend — a wealthy older woman he bragged about sleeping with.

For Sharon, a turning point came the day she went home from the hospital with her three-day-old baby.

"I had a cesarean birth, and I was in a lot of pain," she remembers. "I paid off the cab with the last money I had and, carrying my son, limped up the stairs to our apartment.

"My boyfriend had moved out while I was in the hospital. He'd left me a note on the coffee table, but no money. The rent was overdue. The only food in the house was a package of old soup mix. I sat on the sofa thinking, *I can't go on like this. I have a son to take care of now. I have to do something with my life.*"

Sharon knew she had to resolve the childhood conflicts that had caused her to choose an abusive partner. When I was abusing alcohol, I had such low self-esteem that I went out with anyone who asked me. In sobriety, working a program of recovery, I changed as I began the adventure of discovering who I really was.

In recovery, you will begin to feel that you have the right to a lot of good things, including, if you choose, a loving relationship that is mutually supportive.

In sobriety, in fact, the need for new, healthy choices can become a challenge in itself. After nine years of a bad marriage, Terry is now wondering what *she* wants. She feels unsure about rushing into a sexual relationship with Jeff. She knows she'd like to keep seeing him. He's a very attractive man. But she can hardly say to him, "Do you mind going on hold for about a year while I find out who I am?"

If you are still married when you begin to recover, you will find that a whole new dynamic emerges in your relationship — that a balancing act begins as you change in recovery.

Relationships Are One of the Slipperiest Places of All

Closely tied in with our relationships is our

Emotional Conditioning

> *I learned at an early age that I never wanted to be like my mother. My father treated her like one of the children. His word was law. The first time I ever really stood up for myself — I was sixteen, and we were having an argument because I'd left the iron on — he kicked me out of the house. Later, he said I could come back. But we always had to do things his way.*
>
> — Pat, twenty-seven
> A civil engineer in recovery for twenty-two months

❋   ❋   ❋

Not all of us grew up emotionally conditioned to see men as more important than women. But many of us, *particularly those from alcoholic families*, were conditioned to feel this way. My father, as my opening story in the Arizona trailer park illustrates, was the dominant one in our household. He *ruled* us. And my mother was too weak, too ill, to be any kind of a role model for me. Most of the time I just resented her.

"Keep Daddy Smiling" was the motto around our house. Or, at least, keep Daddy from exploding with anger so that he won't hit anybody. I learned early that doing things for my father — ironing his shirts, winning prizes in school so he could boast about me to his friends — made him notice me. Sometimes it even made him praise me. This, I figured, meant he loved me.

These parameters formed my earliest relationships with men. What I had learned from my antagonistic, belligerent, domineering father was that I was what I *did*. Accomplishments and work were all that counted. I kept up this perpetual tap dance that I'd begun to try to win praise and attention from him.

I was, of course, in a lot of trouble.

If you constantly put your own needs in second place, there will never be time to meet them. Eventually, you'll have no idea what your own needs are. And this is where many of us are when we get sober.

In recovery, we may need new definitions of the word *selfish*. We need role models. By learning to be selfish, we have a chance to genuinely meet the needs not only of our family, husband, employer, and friends, but our own needs as well.

Taking care of everyone's needs before our own doesn't result just in our being tired or stressed out; it results in a tremendous buildup of anger. A buildup of aggression that, sooner or later, we are going to act out somewhere, somehow.

Alcohol and drugs helped us control our anger. And our emotional conditioning (and, for many of us, the abuse we endured as children) made us turn that anger inward.

Often, women turn this anger inward — not even consciously knowing what they've done. That's what substance abuse is: a form of suicide and self-aggression.

Some alcoholic women act out this aggression on other people too. On their children. On their husbands. Guilt, anger, frustration, and fear spiral.

There comes a point for all of us where we desperately want to stop taking our anger out on ourselves and others. At this point, we can be seething volcanos!

Most of us reach this point in early sobriety, and it's a very slippery one for us.

> **We May Feel We Want to Drink Again
> Rather than Face This Anger That Is So Terrifying.**

We're back to bouncing up against society's expectations of us again for the slippery place of

Dual Role Stress

> *Reality is so daily.*
>
> — NANCY LOU, sixty-three

> *At one point, when I was going to school full time, supporting myself and my two babies with almost no help from my ex, my sister and her husband came over. First, I watched him run his finger over the dust on my stereo. Then he wiped the rim of his glass with his handkerchief. He didn't say a word, but his message to me was so clear!*
>
> — DIANE, twenty-eight
> Now finishing her studies
> and beginning a relation-
> ship with a man she met in
> Al-Anon group

* * *

One of the big problems for alcoholic women is that when we get sober, the stress of life is still there. *Life* is still there!

We couldn't cope with life on life's terms before, but at least we could soften the edges of reality with alcohol and other substances. Or maybe we went from man to man as our flight from reality. Our coping patterns were tied into our patterns of abuse. When we get sober, we may discover that we have less energy for coping, and, in some ways, we have less support too. The battle is still going on, but we may feel that we have less ammunition.

You would have thought you'd have more!

And you will.

Several successful recovering alcoholic women have told me that the foundation of their business success has come from what they learned in recovery, in a Twelve Step program. But success in sobriety isn't measured by making a lot of money. It also doesn't mean you marry a man who makes $150 an hour or who looks like Mel Gibson. And it doesn't mean you star on the "Oprah" show. (Although all these things might sound great!)

Success in recovery is getting through one day at a time, taking risks, and putting yourself first.

It's the success of meeting life head on!

CHAPTER TWO

The Way We Were: "Daddy's Girl"

My father was everything to me. Ha, that shows you how small my dreams were! I'd stop dead in my tracks when I heard his car drive up after work. If he was drinking "a little" he'd be in a good mood, and we'd run to him for a hug. If he'd crossed over, all hell would break loose.

— MARGIE, thirty-seven
Active in ACA

My mother was so much against me, she was constantly pointing out all my faults to my dad. I worshipped and adored my father. My childhood idea was that if my father deserted me I would die. So I had to win him over in order to survive.

— MARJORIE, sixty-four
A mathematician

* * *

The scene is now New Mexico, a house on the edge of the desert. Six years have passed since that day in the trailer park when I overheard two neighbors talking about my mother's drinking. Now my mother is dead.

It's a Saturday morning. I'm fifteen, tall for my age, standing at the kitchen sink, breathing in the smell of Palmolive as I wash the breakfast dishes. Through the window, I can see my father and my eight-year-old brother Jimmy, digging post holes to make a fence. The dusty ground shimmers with heat. Their shirts cling damply to their backs.

Jimmy is the baby of the family and everyone's favorite. He's a beautiful boy, golden-haired, and cheerful. From the way my father is shaking his fist, I can tell that Jimmy's work isn't pleasing him. It isn't good enough. The three of us kids are always doing work that isn't good enough, that doesn't measure up to my father's impossibly high standards. We go to school with black eyes, with huge bruises, but no one in authority has ever questioned us about this.

The dishwater gurgles slowly down the drain. A small brown lizard darts across the window ledge. I see Jimmy turn his back on my father. My father's face contorts with anger. He raises his shovel and, swinging it like a baseball bat, smashes it down into Jimmy's spine.

Suddenly everything is noise . . . confusion . . . screaming.

Jimmy is down on the sun-baked ground, on his back, screaming with pain. My father kneels next to him. The muscles of his face look drawn and tight. For once, he seems shocked with the reality of what he's done.

"Daddy! We'd better call an ambulance," I gasp as I race toward them.

"No! No . . . he'll be all right. He's faking it. Shut up, Jimmy. Quit making that goddamned racket." My father's eyes flicker to the house on the left of us to see if anyone is watching. I can guess what he's thinking. No one must know about this.

He does call an ambulance though. He and I stand at the gate watching, as it takes Jimmy, and the story of his "self-inflicted accident," away, alone, to the hospital. My feelings are very mixed. Part of me is scared. Is Jimmy's back broken? Will he be paralyzed?

But a part of me escapes into the drama. I would have liked to have gone with Jimmy in the ambulance, holding his hand, in the role of devoted big sister. Maybe at the hospital somebody would say to me, "Hey, come on — what *really* happened here?" If they forced me to tell the truth, then I wouldn't be responsible for telling tales. We'd be rescued from our father's brutality.

"He brought it on himself," my father says. He sighs. "Goddammit, if you kids would *listen* properly, we wouldn't have all these problems." He turns and strides back to the row of post holes and begins digging furiously. Over his shoulder, he shouts, "Don't you have housework to do?"

"Yes, Daddy."

The ambulance is now just a tiny speck in the distance. I turn and go back inside the house.

* * *

My family background certainly isn't typical of all women who grow up to become alcoholics and addicts. But most of us, men and women alike, come from families that are dysfunctional to some degree. I haven't met an alcoholic woman who doesn't describe some form of abuse and a lot of early childhood despair.

There are many kinds of abuse a child can face at home. There is

Verbal Abuse

You see these children in places like supermarkets being towed along by a mother who is saying, "You're so stupid, Caroline! I don't know what I'm going to do with you! Why can't you ever get *anything* right? You're driving me crazy!"

Terry was abused in this manner, although to outsiders, her home might have looked like a very good one. Terry's mother, by never accepting anything Terry did as good enough, constantly demeaned her.

Margie, whose quote about her father begins this chapter, was also emotionally damaged in this way. Margie, who manages a debt-relief service, began going to ACA meetings after a series of destructive relationships with men:

> *Boy, could I pick 'em. If a guy came after me, you could predict he hated women. My pattern was to be sweet and submissive. With my first and second husbands, I was a complete slave. I worked at a demanding job, cooked, cleaned, and was a great lover — only to be told what a loser I was. I believed them. They made me feel totally inadequate — a failure at marriage and a loser at life.*
>
> *In time, I began to hear those same words from my father's mouth. That was how he had talked to my mother — and then to me. It hit me that the men in my life were just like my father! Oh, no — right out of a Psych 101 textbook! But it was true.*
>
> *My father never hit me, but he was so cruel with his words. He would ridicule and humiliate my mom, and when she was reduced to tears, he'd turn on me. And, because I loved him, I believed him.*

* * *

Bitter fighting between the parents — the kind of fights where the home rings with phrases such as, "I must have been out of my mind to have three kids with a low-life pond scum like you! — is verbal child abuse.

Sometimes, as in the quote from Pat B. that follows, verbal abuse can be very subtle.

> *My father used to say "You love your Daddy, don't you?" He'd say this after arguments, and fighting — and I hated it! But I'd always agree. He'd twist my own words and thoughts and use them as weapons. And they hurt just like fists.*

* * *

I remember so many times in my own childhood when my father called me stupid. Anyone who made a mistake was stupid. While it doesn't seem like much of a form of abuse today, it was devastating to me because that was his most cruel insult — that someone was stupid.

I know it relates a great deal to my adult behavior of not being able to admit I'm wrong or not allowing myself to make a mistake. I'm terrorized by that memory of his voice shouting, "You're stupid — you stupid idiot!"

Another form is

Being Ignored and Neglected

There are families in which the only way for a child to get attention is to do something dramatic, such as breaking a leg. And the little girl who has constant accidents in order to be noticed, may carry it through to become the fourteen-year-old who gets pregnant, and, beyond that, to become the neighborhood "drama queen."

She's the one of whom people may say, *"Everything* happens to that poor woman!" Many alcoholic women, at one time or another, play the role of drama queens.

* * *

I always felt that everything would be fine if only I was perfect.

— LEIGH, twenty-seven

* * *

Carla, a laboratory technician in her late thirties, has been clean and sober for six years. She tells the following story:

In one month, everything had happened to me. My car had been hit by a bus and, because traffic was stalled for blocks, it made the TV news. My son had been accused

25

*of stealing and then broke his arm in a Little League game.
My husband's homeless alcoholic sister and her two children had come to live with us "temporarily," and also my
father who was close to death from emphysema.*

*Then my cat — can you top this! — got hit by a car
the same day my superior announced our federal funding
at the lab had been cut and there would soon be layoffs.*

*How could I connect any of these freaky accidents to
my own drinking?*

*Yet today I know this is the "unmanageability" that
the First Step addresses. Boy, was my life unmanageable!*

* * *

Danielle, thirty-one, is an artist who drives a cab. In early
sobriety, two years ago, the biggest obstacle she encountered,
without alcohol or other drugs, was being alone. She says:

*I gradually began to remember that my mom would
meet my dad after work in a bar down the street. He
worked on an assembly line, and when he got off he'd call
from the bar, and she'd leave. She'd always tell me,
"Don't leave this house, Danielle. No matter what."*

*I'd be terrified that something horrible was going to
happen. I'd picture the house catching on fire and wonder
if I could leave it then. I'd see myself — I was totally
obedient and submissive then — burning to death in order
to obey her.*

*And the terror didn't end when they got home. Usu-
ally it was very late. They'd just go to their bed. Sometimes my dad would only make it as far as the couch before
he passed out.*

*I remember it was almost lonelier with them home
than when they were gone. So I'd spend most evenings
huddled in my room, sometimes sitting at the window
watching other people, but mostly just being afraid — so
afraid.*

Then I learned about getting attention. I'd pretend to be sick, and that worked for a while. Then I'd start telling a big tale just to keep my mother at home for a few more minutes. I'd start a huge lie about something that happened at school or to one of my mother's friends. Or I'd tell her the roof was leaking. Anything to keep her focused on me and to push away the inevitable.

Sometimes I'd run to the window and shout, "Look out! . . ." — pretending an accident was about to happen.

Well, of course, she began to call me a liar and laugh at me. And she'd leave anyway.

I'll bet you can guess the rest. In relationships with men, whenever it looked as though we were going to break up, I'd begin some big dramatic story. I'd say that I'd just lost my job, or I'd just discovered my mother was terminally ill. Sometimes it would be a fatal illness of my own that had just been diagnosed! I'd say anything just to keep the guy with me a little longer.

Achievements are another way a child gets attention. The little girl who takes this route usually gets straight A's . . . wins awards . . . then wins bigger awards. As girls are often expected to take on more domestic chores than boys, she often assumes back-breaking responsibilities. As she continues to try to win everyone's approval, she grows up trying to be Superwoman, possibly a workaholic — as well as an alcoholic.

I remember hearing my recovering friend Deanne talk about how she felt when she started school. She loved it. After the chaos of her family, school was a breeze. There were rules for achieving and gaining approval. I had exactly that same sense of relief about school. At last, I knew how to get the praise and positive attention I craved so desperately.

I had never experienced unconditional love in my home, growing up, and wouldn't until I came to the fellowship of recovery. I learned that love doesn't depend on what you *do*, or do for someone else. As my friend Vickie says, "I'm a human *being*, not a human *doing*."

And, of course, there is the all too common

Physical Abuse

My alcoholic father's physical abuse always took the form of disciplining us but, at some point, his anger and frustration bottled up inside him took over. Fury replaced reason. I can remember him beating Jimmy's bare legs with a rubber hose while Jimmy, age eighteen months, tried to crawl across the trailer away from him, and my mother sobbed helplessly on the couch.

My father was abused as a small child. His father used to beat him, lock him inside a dark closet, and yell through the door, "I'm telling the bogeyman to come and get you."

When he told us the story of the closet and the bogeyman, my father made a joke of it, trivializing it. The story of the day he broke Jimmy's back with a shovel (years after the event, when Jimmy was walking around quite normally) became another story he told in a joking way over a few drinks to friends. "Jimmy was so bad I had to hit him with a goddammed shovel. . . ." He legitimized it, discounting the pain and horror.

This type of thing can be part of the craziness of growing up in an alcoholic family. When you hear somebody telling a tragic story as a joke, you begin to minimize your own responses to that tragedy. Those of us who grow up with this type of distortion learn to tolerate such a high level of insanity that it adds to our inability to distinguish what is real.

* * *

I will no longer be a willing participant in my own abuse.

— My own words,
spoken to Patt

* * *

Carmen is a compulsive overeater, now in recovery and happily married to a recovering alcoholic. She knows now that food was associated with love in her dysfunctional home. It was the way her parents "made up" with her.

> *Both my parents beat me, and my brother and sister. It didn't matter who was at fault, we all got it. They'd use their hands, fists, belts, anything that was close by. I thought all children were treated like this, but I couldn't figure out why I never saw other parents hitting their children.*
>
> *Today when I look at my own little ones, I can't believe what my life was like. It's a wonder I'm not completely looney, because it was so crazy. Especially when we'd be sobbing in our room and my mom would bring some cookies in and tell us to shut up, everything was all right.*

Emotional Incest

The most serious of all the abuses, sexual abuse, wasn't a part of my own childhood. But it wasn't until I'd been in recovery for almost six years that I realized that I'd been — like many, many alcoholic women — a victim of emotional incest. It was one of the biggest insights of my sobriety.

Many people have never heard of emotional incest. It's a distortion of the sexual roles between parent and child. (And it can happen between mothers and sons.)

My insight about it happened when I was chatting casually with my friend Dominic. I'd been talking about the problems I had with long-term relationships with men and how they never seemed to measure up to my expectations. And I began, quite suddenly, to see how I had played a role of wife and mother — failing at both.

By then, my mother was bedridden most of the time. She was in pain. She was coughing. She was drugged. Things were very difficult. I was the caretaker for my father and two brothers. And all this was happening right at the stage when I was turning from a skinny child into a woman. Without knowing it, I was becoming the woman of our family.

But in our strange, alcoholic household my father's way of handling it was to react with even more violent anger and abuse. And the angrier he got, the harder I tried to please him. I was trying to be his "wife" because, obviously, being his child didn't please him.

My friend Andrea once told me of her father's reaction to her at this stage of her life. She and her father had a little ritual after school. He would pick her up by her arms and swing her around like an airplane, with her feet flying out.

Then, one day he came to meet her after school. She ran to meet him and, with a very strange look on his face, he just thrust her away. No explanation. No words at all. They never played the game again.

It's very normal, in childhood development, for a father to be attracted to his daughter. In a normal family, the way that a father reacts is to think something like, *Wow! My little gal's becoming a woman. I've got to give her more privacy.* Or he might talk to his wife about it, and say something like, "She's growing up. I just hate the thought of some man putting his hand on her."

This is how a normal, healthy man should handle this. He understands that she is not the woman for him. Some fathers, in fact, pass through this stage unaware that they have passed through it.

This distortion of the roles between father and daughter happens often in alcoholic families where there are many inappropriate examples of sexual acting out.

Exhibitionism is another form. Sandra remembers:

> My father would walk around the house in his under-wear. I never thought it strange that the minute he got home from work, he would strip down to his shorts. They were baggy boxer shorts — nothing "erotic," but I know from my earliest memories I didn't like seeing him that way, and I'd turn my head.

Whether he knew it consciously or not, Sandra's father was acting out sexual attraction — emotional incest, without touching.

Denise, now thirty-two, describes another form:

> *When my father and I are alone all he wants to talk about is Mom and her faults and how bad his marriage is. It's like I'm the wife, and she's a child we're discussing. It's been this way for so long it seems normal to me. I'm the wife, and Mom's the bad little girl.*
>
> *In the last five years, since Dad retired, he's called me almost daily to talk about domestic stuff — what's wrong with Mom, or that dinner was late, or should he change insurance companies? . . . on and on. I was so conditioned I just kept listening.*
>
> *Therapy was extremely critical to my recovery and Co-Dependents Anonymous meetings have helped a lot, but I'm beginning to feel the anger of being abused all these years. I alternate between feeling rage and then sadness for how dysfunctional my family was — and is.*

Marjorie's father subjected her to another form of emotional incest — *without ever touching her* — when she was in her teens:

> *He took me to a bankers' convention in Chicago, and passed me off as his girlfriend to his buddies. I went along with it because I could see that it was a game he wanted to play. When he finally confessed to his friends that I was his daughter, it was all a great big joke.*
>
> *But I remember feeling very peculiar about his saying I was his girlfriend. It was about that time that he let me know that he had girlfriends and that he wasn't faithful to my mother. It was a terrible thing for me to know because it made me suspicious of all men.*

31

The form of childhood abuse that brings out the strongest denials of all (usually among all members of the family) is the "secrets in the dark," one of

Sexual Abuse

Leah, thirty-eight, is now a nurse in an intensive care ward. She says:

> *I was eight the day my grandfather followed me into the woods. He was a huge man, about six-four, with a violent temper. I was scared of him. He had been coming to my bedroom and doing sexual things to me for about a year, but he had never gone as far as actual intercourse.*
>
> *Then one day my grandfather found me in the woods. I heard his voice booming out: "Leah, I want to show you a surprise." He took my hand and led me toward a thick clump of bushes.*
>
> *When he pulled me on top of him, I was terrified! I managed, somehow, to break free and run back to the house. I was shaking all over. Who could I tell? Who would believe me? I sat down in a corner and pretended to be reading a magazine. My aunt Jean came in and said, "My, your mind must be on something else. You're holding that magazine upside down!" Then she chuckled and went away. She didn't ask me if anything was wrong.*
>
> *My experiences with my grandfather left me with a tremendous fear, and many times a rage, that was projected to men. I panicked when a relationship started getting intimate.*
>
> *I don't think I realized until recently how deep the scars went. I married a pilot who often got home from work in the middle of the night. One night he came in, found me sleeping in our bed, and bent over me to kiss my forehead.*

*"You had such a strange reaction," he told me the
next morning. "You pulled the covers up to your chin
and clamped your lips shut."*

*Yet, for most of my adult life I minimized the sexual
abuse. That's typical. Incest can be just like alcoholism.
There's a lot of denial.*

Leah's story has not ended, but professional help plus
Twelve Step meetings and support groups have helped her
recover.

How often does sexual abuse happen to female children?
Statistics differ, but all the recent studies show that the numbers are staggeringly high. Seventy-four percent of the
women alcoholics who took part in a recent study by San
Diego psychologist Stephanie Covington had been sexually
abused as children. In another study, it was 80 percent.

If left untreated, sexual abuse damages not only a woman's
sexual history, but her entire life.[*]

* * *

*There's a lot of guilt. I used to be overwhelmed by it.
It haunted me. In many ways it was the deepest, darkest
secret of my life. My alcoholism was the second secret.*
— ANDREA, forty-two
A commercial realtor

* * *

Andrea was sexually abused by her uncle between the
ages of seven and eleven. He was quite brazen about it, often
abusing her inside the house while the entire family was outside talking around the pool.

---

[*] It is important for any woman who has been or suspects she has
been abused to seek professional help.

Andrea told no one. For Andrea, part of her recovery involved confronting her uncle about the sexual abuse. She says:

> *In recovery, I've grown to recognize that it's just a part of my history. But it took me three years of recovery before I felt this way. I had to work the Twelve Steps of the program twice.*
>
> *The first person I told was my sponsor, after she had told of her own experience of incest. I was thirty-eight. When I told my mother, she was horrified and very supportive. When I decided to confront my uncle, I arranged to see him, and then I couldn't sleep. I couldn't eat. I was too nervous to go to work. I remember what his exact words were. He said, "God, I hoped in my heart that you had forgotten it."*
>
> *I still have dreams about it. I still have a hard time letting my six-year-old daughter spend the night with friends. But I no longer blame incest for my alcoholism. It was only a part of it. One of the pieces.*
>
> *Today I look at what has happened to me as a gift, because if I hadn't been through what I have, I wouldn't be able to help other women. I'm now a sponsor to a woman in her mid-forties who recently told me about the incest in her family, and she was speaking of it for the first time.*

So, one way or another, many of us grow up in homes filled with secrets. In homes where reality is often strangely twisted. We learn early to tolerate high levels of abuse. Many of us become little workhorses. We live with guilt and shame.

And no matter what type of home we come from — dysfunctional, violent, or so-called normal — those of us who become alcoholic grow up feeling that we're different. Some women speak of feeling "like an alien from another planet."

I always felt that I was different. I felt that there was some secret to life that everybody else knew. Some secret that I just couldn't seem to grasp.

Have you been able to identify with some form of childhood abuse? The damage is frequently subtle. Without some kind of help in healing, years later the abuse can show up in your life as you

- try to be perfect, a Superwoman.
- people-please.
- feel guilty about saying no.
- become a professional and perpetual caretaker.
- abuse others, in the same ways you were abused.
- end up being a doormat.

Drinking and using other chemicals can blunt the pain of this way of life. They can become our survival technique.

❋ ❋ ❋

Made a searching and fearless moral inventory of ourselves.
> — The Fourth Step
> From the Twelve Steps of
> Alcoholics Anonymous

❋ ❋ ❋

It's midnight. Except for the distant sound of a dog barking, Terry's house is quiet. Peaceful. She sits cross-legged on "her" side of the king-sized bed. It's the same bed that she and Ben, her ex-husband, charged to his MasterCard only three days before their wedding. Am I, *she wonders,* ever going to learn to sleep in the middle of it?

She smiles at the thought of the picture she must present. Ben would hate it! The faded, comfortable sleep-shirt, patterned with pandas, pulled up over the too-white skin of her thighs. The clutter of self-help books on "his" side.

The pen in her hand moves swiftly as she scribbles in her notebook. Already tonight she has written twelve pages. What am I doing, *she wonders.* Writing a novel, on my Fourth Step?

Terry looks over the list she's been making. People she has resentments toward. She smiles. Her mother is the first on the list. Terry has just visited her today. Her mind begins to replay the scene. Her mother's words, spoken earlier that day in the kitchen, keep echoing, distracting her.

". . . letting Ben go was the stupidest thing. . . ."

"I don't care for your hair tied back that way. It simply doesn't suit you."

"Are you putting on weight?"

There had been more of the same endless criticism during dinner. Her mother felt Terry wasn't taking care of the kids properly. She was doing too much. She was doing too little. . . .

Has, she wonders, her mother always been this critical? So judgmental? So carelessly cruel? The answer, Terry realizes, is yes!

* * *

In sobriety, working the Steps allows us to come to grips with childhood (and adult) abuse.

As Terry began to use the Fourth Step, she wrote down the words her mother had often punished her with. Gradually, as memories came flooding back, she began to write down similar things she remembered saying to Ben. Suddenly, she realized that she had said them to her children too! God forbid! Was she getting to be just like her mother?

That night, Terry realized that this thing called a Fourth Step was a lot more than she had bargained for. She wrote furiously for hours — wanting to get it all out, wanting to move on. Wanting to get well.

There are many ways we can confront the abuses of our past. We can accomplish a lot just by the simple process of sharing our secrets in meetings — by sharing with others who understand some of what we've been through.

Marilyn was one of my first role models in sobriety. I first noticed her because she was exceptionally pretty. But it was her powerful message that kept my attention. It was from her that I first heard the philosophy that we are "only as sick as our secrets."

Marilyn was in her early thirties, with about seven years of sobriety. She belonged to what I saw as a small exclusive clique of very attractive women who hung out together at meetings. That was the way I saw them, but they weren't really a clique. I came to realize that they were just recovering women who wanted to spend time together. All of them appeared to be successful in every way. I was still judging my insides — how I felt — by their outsides — how they looked.

At that time, my own career was sort of a "zero." I felt *I* was sort of a zero too. I felt that I had no value as a human being. I can remember gazing wistfully across the room at Marilyn and her friends and thinking, *They're all so terrific. They won't want to know me.*

It was rather like being back in high school and envying the "in" crowd! Of course, later, when I got to know these women, I discovered that they had the same problems as everybody else. That they, too, were battling the "looking good" myth, along with low self-esteem.

One night, Marilyn and her friend Mara asked me if I would like to join them for dinner.

I was thrilled! *Wow!* I thought, *I've* arrived.

Over dinner, Marilyn talked with candor and humility about an incestuous relationship she'd had with her brother. Over time, I was to hear her share this secret many times — in both open and mixed meetings. She was always direct. Always honest. I saw that she was proof that sharing your secrets worked because of the success of her sober life.

Sometimes, professional help is needed in recovery. Frequently, amends must be made. Whatever path you choose, begin today. Like Marilyn, I've shared all my secrets in meetings and with my sponsor. By giving up the terrible burden of secrets, I'm no longer collaborating in my own abuse.

CHAPTER THREE

Our Bodies:
Healthy at Last?

Lower your standards if you are compulsive about housework. You don't have to polish the doorknobs to prove you're a good person.
                    — From *The Women's Health Source*
                                        Scripps Memorial
                                        Hospital, San Diego

* * *

Terry sits at the counter in her mother's gleaming kitchen, feeling her temples pounding with the pain of a headache. Another one! Maybe she's getting so many of them because she hasn't been sleeping well? Although it's Sunday and only noon, she feels exhausted.

"You married one of the nicest men God ever made," her mother is saying, as she slaps a chicken breast aggressively into a mound of seasoned flour. Soft white flour particles rise in the warm kitchen air. "I'm telling you, Terry, letting Ben go was the stupidest thing you ever did."

"Mom, he divorced me. He said that after I quit drinking I wasn't the same per...."

"Yeah, yeah," her mother mutters — cutting her off in mid-sentence. "Pass me that roll of paper towels would you, Sweetie?"

A burst of laughter floats in from the patio where her father is showing Beth and Cody how to give the dog what he calls "Grandpop's Superwash." As Terry reaches for the paper towels, she feels the waistband of her shorts biting into her waist. She must have put on at least ten pounds since she quit taking diet pills! When she was drinking, the alcohol had always taken the edge off her appetite. Now it seems like she's hungry all the time.

Hungry for things like chocolate chip cookies. She loves to eat them warm, topped with gently melting vanilla ice cream. Most of her social life these days revolves around her recovery group, and that, too, led to eating sweets. At the end of every meeting, someone was sure to say, "Hey, let's go get some ice cream."

Good grief, *Terry thinks,* I'm always tired, and my house is always a mess, and my lawn's turning yellow because I keep forgetting to water it. I have trouble sleeping. No sex life. And now I'm getting fat!

Was giving up drinking worth it?

Yes! Yes! Of course it was. Sitting on the kitchen stool, carefully groping under her T-shirt and undoing the top button of her shorts, Terry remembers the days when she was having blackouts. All those times when she thought she was going to get fired from her job! She remembers how scared she was. Scared for the kids.

She draws in a deep breath. She smiles at her mother, now busily stuffing chicken breasts into a cooking bag.

"I'm dating a very nice man now, Mom. We've been out twice, to dinner and to a play at the Moonlight Theatre. You'd like him. His name's Jeff. He has his own business."

"Hmmm," her mother murmurs. "I must say I don't care for your hair tied back that way, Terry. It doesn't suit you. Are you putting on weight?"

"Yes."

The need to really confide in her mother sweeps over Terry. She would like, she realized, her mother to take her in her arms, and be warm and comforting and motherly, even though at no time in her life has her mother ever been any of these things.

"Mom. . ." *she begins. Tears seem to be choking her voice.* "Mom, I'm not feeling so great. I don't feel well. I'm so tired."

"Oh, I've got something wonderful for that!" *her mother exclaims. "My girlfriend, Vera — you remember Vera, don't you? The one I go antiquing with. She gave them to me."*

"Not pills, Mom?" *Terry asks.*

But her mother is already heading for her bathroom. As she slides back the glass doors of her bathroom cabinet, Terry sees a rainbow assortment of bottles. An almost-empty bottle of Valium pills is setting on the seafoam green tiles next to the sink.

A saying she has heard at a Twelve Step meeting flashes through Terry's mind. "If I've got an ill, I've got a pill."

"Here!" *her mother is saying. "These orange ones. I'm not even sure what's in them, but they work. Believe me, Sweetie, you'll be cleaning your house at midnight."*

Now Terry stands in the doorway to the bedroom in her too-tight shorts, staring at her mother. A pill for every ill. Quick fix! She can never remember, she realizes, her mother facing any kind of situation — everyday or crisis — without some kind of a quick fix.

Mom's softened the edges of her whole life, *Terry thinks.* Just as I used to do. Why didn't I realize before that she's an addict?

Terry lets her back slide slowly down the bedroom wall, until she is sitting on the hardwood floor of her parent's bedroom with her knees drawn up. The floor smells of lemon oil. It gleams. Does her mother clean it at midnight? Probably.

She sighs. To move, to get back on her feet again, to go out to the patio and join Dad and the kids, seems overwhelmingly difficult.

❋ ❋ ❋

Terry was exhausted because she was growing, gaining in awareness. All of us who are recovering go through days like this. Days when our growing awareness feels overwhelming.

And complicating this is the fact that most of us are surprised by the way our bodies act. If you are a woman new in sobriety, your thoughts may run along the lines of: *What's* happening *here? I'm not drinking now. Surely I should be feeling much better? I feel worse! And why am I getting so many colds? Why is it so hard to concentrate?*

It's typical in early recovery to have days when you wake up feeling wonderful. Euphoric! Capable of coping with almost anything. On other days, you feel so overwhelmed, so tired, that it's an effort just to crawl out of bed and make it as far as the shower.

What Terry needed was simply time.

Time is what all of us need.

It takes a lot of energy to heal, and that energy is pulled from the body. No one's body bounces back overnight after years of substance abuse. In recovery, we likely don't look like a convalescent — no plaster casts, no bandages, or crutches — but a convalescent is exactly what we are.

Another slippery place in new sobriety is that you begin to notice things. Aches and pains, for instance, that may have existed before but, with alcohol, were easy to ignore. You notice flaws in your body that you weren't conscious of earlier. (Especially if, like me, you were drinking around the clock before you hit bottom.)

* * *

One evening, my sister phoned just as I was getting out of the shower. I ran to answer the phone with only a towel clutched around my middle.

There's a long mirror on the wall by my phone, and as I talked I was looking into it. I suddenly realized that I was staring at all these stretch marks. They were all over my thighs. I thought, Oh my God, when did this happen to me? And I'm putting on weight! When did I start to put on weight? This is terrible! *I don't think I heard a word of what my sister was saying to me.*

— SHARON, twenty-six
A college student
with a small son

Booze makes you believe what you want to believe.
— CONNIE, seventy-two

* * *

As alcoholic women, most of us felt that the way our outside looked was very important. We had to look good, because we felt so worthless on the inside. As we begin working a recovery program, we discover that recovery depends on becoming totally comfortable with the way we are. *Just* as we are.

Recovery means

Acceptance

Another challenge in new sobriety is the way we feel about discomfort the first time we get sick.

* * *

A couple of months after I got sober I had a hysterectomy. I remember lying on the sofa, the day I came home from the hospital, thinking, Oh, what wouldn't I give for a glass of wine right now.
— GAIL, early forties

* * *

I have an old whiplash injury. In my drinking days, whenever the pain flared up, I'd simply climb into bed with a Valium and a glass of bourbon. (And probably one of the cheap romance novels I loved to read.) This combination relaxed every muscle in my body. After awhile I'd get up again and go happily back to work.

In early sobriety, however, I was shocked to discover that even a cold made me feel like I was dying! *Surely,* I thought, *a cold never felt this bad before?*

It didn't feel as bad. What I was experiencing, what all of us experience the first time in our recovery that we get sick, was *Sick Sober*.

And the best way to handle this, to be reassured, is to talk to other recovering women about their health-related experiences in recovery.

* * *

The first time I remember drinking alcohol was the day I got my first period. I guess I was about twelve or thirteen. I had terrible cramps. My mom fixed me a small glass of whiskey with honey in it. "Take it with you into a hot bath, Lori," she told me. "It'll relax you." I can still remember how warm and comforting it was. No wonder I continued to turn to alcohol whenever I felt any pain, physically or emotionally.

— LORRAINE, twenty-nine
A repeated slipper, now
sober for three months and
living in a recovery home

* * *

When I was suffering through that first sober cold — and I really did think I was on the verge of death! — my sponsor brought me flowers on a visit. She said she'd felt exactly the same way with her first sober cold. We talked for a long time. And she opened my eyes to the fact that, since early childhood, when my mother used to give me a hot toddy of hot water, bourbon, lemon, and honey, in my mind, that mixture was tied in with having someone love me. With having someone take care of me. Comfort medicine!

In recovery it's important to remember that alcohol wasn't just in our glass. It was in every part of our life.

* * *

In early recovery, the two health-related areas that I had the most *fun* with were sleep and food.

Sleep was a joy. I had been having horrifying, drug-related nightmares while using. Once the drugs were out of my system, falling asleep became a delight for me. It still is.

This isn't everyone's experience though.

> *I always went to bed with a drink in my hand. The first night I quit drinking, I thought,* I haven't been to bed without a drink for eighteen years. How will I ever fall asleep?
>
> — CINDY, forty-one
> A nursing supervisor who
> currently leads retreats for
> recovering women

* * *

In new sobriety, many of us find there is a need to relearn the drifting away that precedes natural sleep. We may need, at first, to try playing gentle meditation tapes to soothe us.

In the early months, you may find that when you lie down in bed your brain starts firing anxiety messages. You may wake up several times in the night with anxiety attacks, or dream that you are drinking again. To dream of drinking is very common.

* * *

> *I was so excited by my first sober birthday. I've slipped, gone back to drinking several times. But this time is different. I feel different. When I went to bed on the night of my birthday, I was feeling so good about myself.*

Then, in my dream, I was in my kitchen pouring myself a large glass of brandy. It was so real! I drank the brandy, and I could taste it.

When I woke up, the taste was still in my mouth, and I thought, Oh, No! I've done it again!

— MEG, in her fifties

* * *

In my first year of sobriety, food was even more of a joy to me than sleep. Much of the time, in the two or three years before I hit bottom, I'd simply forget to eat. On my first day of sobriety, I was so weak that my daughter Deanna had to help me get dressed for my first Twelve Step meeting. Deanna insisted that I stand on the bathroom scales.

"Oh, Mom," she said, "You're only 105 pounds!"

I was gaunt at that weight, since I'm tall.

That first year I had a wonderful time with food. My favorite meal was a big steak, with a big salad on the side, and a huge baked potato smothered in butter or sour cream. And ice cream for dessert. Ice cream is a favorite with many recovering alcoholics. As well as being sweet — and we crave sweetness to replace the sugar we consumed in alcohol — ice cream seems like another "comfort food."

By the end of the year, I was up to 125 pounds. With my height, that was fine. By that time I was looking healthier.

But then I kept on gaining . . . gaining. . . .

Well, I thought, *I'll just do what I've always done whenever I wanted to lose some weight. I'll simply stop eating for three days.* Not a good idea, but this is what I'd always done.

And I did. They were three terrible days!

What I didn't realize is that there's no pain in fasting when you're drinking or using. Any diet is easy then. And, although I hadn't exactly been getting ripped on cocaine every day, I was using it enough to live at a rate of speed that burned calories rapidly.

Nearly everyone in early sobriety either gains or loses weight. Just being aware of this helps. Eventually, as my life became more balanced, my body did too. I learned to adjust to eating smaller portions and healthier foods. And I began exercising.

If you were bloated because of alcohol use, you'll likely lose weight in your first year.

* * *

In my first month, I lost thirty pounds. After six months, I had gone from 197 to 118 pounds. I could wear jeans again! I was thrilled.

— JAN, late forties

* * *

When we get sober, it isn't exactly as if a fairy godmother waves a wand over us and — pow! — in a burst of stardust, we become a whole new person. We're in a process of changing. And most of us still have our obsessive-compulsive natures.

I was such an all-or-nothing personality For me, one of the biggest challenges of early sobriety was learning how to relax. How to pace myself. How to stop trying to be Superwoman.

* * *

Sometimes I think my husband wishes I was drinking again. I had so much energy then. When I was drinking, I had a full-time job and a spotless house. I made all my children's clothes. I made extra money by teaching seminars. Once, I came home from working a full shift and wallpapered two bedrooms. Nobody thought I was an alcoholic. They thought I was some kind of Superwoman.

— CINDY, forty-one

> *A drink was always my treat. Whenever I got tired,*
> *instead of taking a break, I'd pour myself a drink.*
> — PAM, early forties

* * *

How do we get to be Superwoman? Through "supernatural" powers. And those "supernatural" powers come from drugs.

There are many of us, like Cindy, who were whirling through our days on artificial stimulation, usually doing three things at once, overwhelmed and overcommitted. Often, at least in the early stages of our disease, we were admired for our ability to accomplish so much. As Joyce, now sixty, says:

> *When I was about six months sober my daughter said, "You know, Mom, you were a lot more fun when you were drinking." I was always the mother in the neighborhood who did all the carpooling, the baking for fund raisers, taking ten children on overnight camping trips, etcetera. I used to drive, about half-smashed, with all those kids, singing at the top of my voice. It's just a miracle I was never in a wreck.*
>
> *Later, when I went back to work as an executive secretary, I tried to carry on that level of being indispensable to everybody. No one at work realized that I was an alcoholic. I used to carry vodka to the office with me in a large Scope mouthwash bottle. I'd leave just enough of the Scope in to color it blue, in case anyone saw me pulling it out of my purse in the ladies' room.*
>
> *I was used to accomplishing a lot. But my drinking gave me tremendous health problems. My liver was shot. In very early sobriety, two days out of a detoxification center, I knew I wasn't strong enough for the "real world" yet, so I went to sign up at a recovery house for women.*

I couldn't even hold the pen to fill out the form they gave me. I said to the two women there, "I'm so sorry. I'm having a little difficulty." They were both recovering alcoholics. They just smiled and said, "Tell us about it!"

* * *

One of the early recovery difficulties for those of us who tried so hard to be superwomen, is that we often feel too exhausted to do much of anything, let alone all the things we did before.

* * *

I had lots of nervous energy when I was drinking. I used crystal and speed — I was always pumping something into my body. I used to work for a computer company, and when the bars closed at 2:00 A.M., I'd often go back to the office and work. In recovery, one of my biggest problems has been fatigue.

— CAT, twenty-seven
A dispatcher in a fire
station, in recovery for
three years

* * *

As our bodies try to stabilize after withdrawal of alcohol and other drugs, we have a natural and automatic loss of energy. We also have intermittent euphoric periods of energy — a second wind. We're like a runner at the end of a long race.

Feeling This Way Is Normal

Accepting the fact that we can't expect too much of ourselves during this period is a positive step in recovery.

* * *

*I never missed a day of work when I was drinking.
But I was often hungover. Below par. Just getting
through the day. Now, with two and a half years of
sobriety, I'm amazed at how much energy I have. When
you're drinking, it takes a lot of energy just to cover up
how bad you feel.*

— GAIL
A school teacher
in her early forties

* * *

The healthier you are when you begin sobriety, the quicker
you'll snap back. But a slippery place for those of us who used
to try to be Superwomen is that we may carry on our former
pattern. We may still measure our worth in terms of what we
can accomplish.

The art of relaxation is a learned process. So is pacing
ourselves. We get better at slowing our pace with practice. I
discovered this about six months into sobriety. I was just at the
stage where the fog was lifting a little, and I'd heard other
people in the program say that a big part of recovery was
learning how to be good to yourself.

I can be good to myself, I thought. *I'll start by taking a five-
minute relaxation break during the working day.*

The next afternoon, I carefully locked my office door. I lay
down on the couch. I kept my suit jacket on, buttoned up. I
kept my shoes on too.

I suddenly realized that I was laying flat on my back, arms
stiffly by my sides, feet pointing straight up, ready to spring
into action!

As our recovery progresses, we eventually learn how to
relax. But to say, "Well, my dear, you've spent a lot of time
looking after others. Now you must look after yourself," to a
newly recovering woman and expect her to suddenly learn
relaxation, is pointless. It's a little like saying, "Here is a word

processor. Now you can write a book," to a man who has spent his entire life isolated in the depths of the Zaire rain forests.

We hear the words, but we don't understand them.

* * *

Balance is a key word. Leading a balanced life. It's very elusive. In recovery, you're striving to be so many things. And, never having done it right to begin with, there's a lot of trial and error.
— PAM, early forties

* * *

Other challenges encountered in new sobriety are our physical feelings and responses related to sex.

I was confused about sexual feelings. I was scared. Like so many recovering women, I'd never experienced sex without alcohol or other drugs. The thought of going on a date without alcohol — of making love absolutely sober — was frightening.

Research shows that 70 percent of first sexual experiences are connected in some way with alcohol. That doesn't mean people are drunk every time they have sex! It doesn't mean that men have to be drunk to seduce women, or women have to be drunk in order to feel confident enough about sex.

It simply means, I think, that alcohol is so much a part of the normal social life of most people that it is tied in a very special way to sex.

Perhaps you remember from high school the thrill, the adrenaline rush of buying liquor when you were under age? Or stealing it from your parents' liquor cabinet? Because it's taboo, there's often a certain thrill about that first drink that's also connected to sex.

As we mature, it becomes more ritualized, perhaps along the lines of "Let's have a couple of drinks, have dinner, have a

brandy after dinner at my apartment, and then we'll have sex."
For many people it's simply wine with dinner, a cocktail to
relax, and sex a little later. Champagne to celebrate is another
ritual.

There is nothing wrong or bad about any of this. But for
the alcoholic woman, sex and alcohol become entwined. She
may begin to take some shortcuts to intimacy with alcohol.
She may, for instance, discover that if she's feeling too tired for
sex, alcohol perks her up. It works!

Women report almost universally in studies that alcohol
makes them feel sexier, more confident, more of "a woman."
These are all feelings that perhaps could be developed with
getting to really know a partner, with intimacy, and with time.
Using alcohol to create them feeds in very well with our
speeded up society of the quick fix.

Alcoholic women often begin having sex very young.
Many of us confuse sexual feelings with the need to be loved.
If, like me, you grew up in a home where little physical affec-
tion was given to you, you may long to be hugged, to be loved.
As adults, it can become an unspoken exchange: *I'll give you sex
if you'll hold me and make me feel loved.*

❋   ❋   ❋

*The minute you pick up that first drink you pick up a
crutch.*

— JEANNIE, twenty-nine

❋   ❋   ❋

As the years passed and my disease progressed, alcohol
began to create some very negative sexual experiences in my
life — the experiences of promiscuity, of compromise, of poor
judgment. They were all directly tied to alcohol.

The guilt and remorse I felt often led me to making sexual
compromises both in and out of marriage. Sex is a way of

"making up," a way of saying "I'm sorry." It's also a way to be held in someone's arms, to feel loved, secure, and that everything is okay — even when you know that it isn't.

Many women believe as I did, that, for men, affection and sex are inextricably tied together. I believed the only way to get affection from a man was through seduction and flirtation.

If you've altered your feelings around sex for a long time — either to enhance them or to change them — in new sobriety you are not likely to have much confidence around men. Your crutch is gone!

In early recovery, I think all of us have to confront our sexual histories. For some of us, that history took place solely in a monogamous marriage. For some, it was out on the streets. Some of us had relationships in which we made compromises around alcohol, other drugs, and sex. Our integrity and our value systems were violated.

In the first weeks of recovery, when I began to feel and look better again, I didn't know there was anything wrong with the way I related to men. I didn't know that my "old tapes" were not part of the recovery program. And in my first thirty days, I began to date. My new life seemed to be right on track. But I felt very uncomfortable about sex; I felt something was wrong.

I was hesitant about talking about sex with the women I met in the program. I mistakenly thought that I didn't know them well enough.

Fortunately, early in my recovery, a woman I met at a meeting invited me over for dinner. Yvonne had only sixty days more sobriety than I had. When I drove to her place, it was the first time that I'd gone out socially, that I had felt safe enough to go out.

Yvonne barbecued hot dogs on the patio. Then, while her two young daughters got ready for bed, she said, "Let's relax and sit outside." The sun was setting. It was that lovely, quiet time of the evening when there are few traffic sounds. We were both silent, deep in our thoughts.

Then, out of the blue, Yvonne said, "You know, a couple of things happened to me when I first got sober, Ann. For a while I was completely asexual. I didn't want to do anything. I didn't even want to masturbate. And I worried about that."

"You did?" I said. I'd been worrying about that too. Along with worrying about dating, I'd been wondering if I was ever again going to have any sexual feelings.

"Oh, yes," Yvonne said. "But then I went through a phase where I wanted to get laid by anything that moved."

"Ah," I murmured. She hadn't asked me if anything like this was happening to me, but I somehow felt that she knew I was confused. By sharing her experience with me, her words gave me permission to feel whatever was right for me at that particular time.

I felt as though a little light had gone on in my head, illuminating the words *however I feel sexually is okay*.

This conversation with Yvonne, plus a terrible date I had soon after, led to my decision to be celibate for my first year of sobriety.

For me, that was the right choice. I wasn't in touch with my body or my emotions enough to be in a physically intimate relationship with a man. To become emotionally hooked to a man. I had too much recovering to do before I would become involved in any way.

What Are We Recovering from Physically?

In recovery, we're responsible for our health, for our physical and emotional recovery. To be fully responsible though, it's important that we know what it is that we're recovering from.

Today professionals understand a great deal about the contributing factors of alcoholism:

- *Your Family History:* There's a large body of research now verifying a genetic link. Alcoholism is often passed on from generation to generation. Another contributing factor is that parents teach by example. If your parents used alcohol to deal with stress, as well as any other emotional responses — joy, sorrow, pain, celebration — you are likely to learn to cope this way too.

- *The Biological Organism — You:* Along with the studies on genetic transmission, research shows that many alcoholics have unique physiological characteristics. There is new evidence that alcoholics metabolize alcohol differently than nonalcoholics — that we may be *allergic* to alcohol. But simply, putting aside medical jargon and scientific data, as the Big Book says, "Most of us have been unwilling to admit we were real alcoholics. No person likes to think he is bodily and mentally different from his fellows."

- *Stress:* Stress is what we, as addicts and alcoholics, handle with the aid of substances. Most of us have had highly stressful lives from the beginning, especially if alcoholism was in the family. Inappropriate ways of coping with stress are the downfall of the alcoholic.

Early recovery can be very stressful. If you are in new recovery, you may feel overwhelmed. You may feel the way Terry feels at the beginning of this chapter. But it must be one foot in front of the other, and One Day at a Time. Terry and I began, just as you began. Your own beginning comes each morning.

✱ ✱ ✱

Health in recovery is a gradual process of self-education and experience with sobriety. Most of us, as our drinking grew more and more out of control, tried many different things. We tell a lot of jokes in meetings about our various health "therapies": We may have tried being a vegetarian, drinking only on weekends, getting hypnotized, having acupuncture, going to a psychiatrist, or moving to Hawaii.

When I was drinking — and downing my daily vitamins with a beer or a glass of wine — I had a whole shelf full of books about nutrition, exercise, and health. Sometimes I even read a page or two. Then one day, about six months into sobriety, I noticed the book *Our Bodies Ourselves*, by the Boston Women's Collective, in my bookcase.

Oh, I thought, *I don't think I've ever read that all the way through.* So I did. And it was wonderful. It was as though in sobriety I was reading with new eyes. I was seeing with a new perspective. Reading became one step for me in the process of self-education, of learning to take care of myself.

Beyond reading, I began to realize that I had a world of resources — books, people, experiences, and a program. I was no longer alone.

CHAPTER FOUR

In the Shadows: Stigma

I was dating this guy who was really nice, but he didn't want me to tell his family I was an alcoholic. He kept saying "But you're not! Maybe you used to be one, but you don't drink at all now."

— CAT, twenty-seven

After I got sober, the whole time my husband and I were still married, about ten years, he only went to two meetings. One was when I got my first year cake. He didn't even want to go then. He didn't want anybody to see him going to an AA meeting because they might think <u>he</u> was the alcoholic and ruin his reputation.

— MARINA, forty three
Married to a physician
for twenty years

* * *

Silver and white balloons rustle in the branches of the Monterey pine tree above Terry's head. Soft murmurs of conversation drift around her as she sits on a folding chair beside Jeff in his parent's garden, waiting for the wedding of his youngest sister to begin. Someone has overwatered the grass. The legs of their chairs are sinking slowly downward.

Fifty yards in front of them, a young man in a white tuxedo is perched on a stool, under an arch trimmed with white carnations, playing a guitar and singing a song about promises.

"That's the bridegroom. Glen. He's something of a ham," Jeff murmurs. "He wrote that song himself. They'll probably have to get him off with a hook." He reaches over and clasps one of her hands. "Love you," he whispers.

Terry manages a smile. She feels gritty-eyed with exhaustion. She was up most of the night with Cody, who has the flu. She has a deadline on Monday for an article about how conventioneers spend their money, and she hasn't even begun the research. Her mind keeps replaying a conversation she and Jeff had three nights ago. It was the first time she had told him that she was a recovering alcoholic.

She hears, again, his voice saying, "An alcoholic? How can you be an alcoholic? I've never even seen you have one drink." Then her own voice, explaining that this was a disease that could be arrested, but never cured. It wasn't going to go away. If she never drank again, she would still be a recovering alcoholic for the rest of her life.

Then Jeff, sounding uneasy, asking her to be careful not to mention her alcoholism to his family when she met them at the wedding.

"Jeff, I wasn't planning to. Why would I tell them? It's not usually a subject that comes up in casual conversation. You know, like, 'Hasn't the weather been nice lately? And did I happen to mention that I'm a recovering addict?'"

"Terry, I'm serious. They wouldn't understand. No one in our family has ever been alcoholic."

She's an embarrassment to him! What would happen if she actually married him? Would he feel the same about his business clients finding out that his wife is a recovering alcoholic? Would he, as Ben used to do, want her to hide the fact that she went to AA? It could go on and on. . . .

This relationship with Jeff is just not going to work. He's younger and more open-minded than Ben. He's nicer than Ben. But, just like Ben, he seems to have trouble believing she is an alcoholic.

Glen is still singing, something about being true. The bride, Karin, a dazzle of white and silver in the sunlight, is walking around the corner of the house on the arm of her father.

Terry feels a twinge of . . . not envy, exactly. No, not envy, because she is genuinely happy for Karin. Maybe wistfulness describes her feelings better. She can barely remember her own wedding. That whole day passed in a Valium-softened blur.

*   *   *

The minister is reading the words of the ceremony. Has the bridegroom written those too? Jeff's knee is pressing against hers. The jacket of her cream-linen suit feels tight, as if a button might ping off at any moment.

"And do you, Glen Callum Robertson, take this woman. . . ."

There would be toasts later. There were always toasts at a wedding. Should she ask for her usual drink, Diet Pepsi? How was it going to look — everyone holding a glass of champagne, and there she'd be, holding aloft a can of Pepsi?

Suddenly the people around her are rising. The ceremony is over. The minister's bald spot is sun-flushed to a rosy pink. Terry looks down and sees that one of her suit buttons is hanging by a thread.

"Now I can introduce you to all the family you haven't met yet," Jeff is saying. "See that woman in the red-feathered hat over there? That's an aunt of mine who's a children's book editor. You two should have a lot in common — both being in the writing business."

"I'll just make a quick trip to the bathroom first," Terry murmurs, feeling thankful that she always carries a miniature sewing kit in her purse. It was one advantage of having been reared by a perfectionist mother.

Her head is pounding with another headache. In Jeff's parents' bedroom, she swallows two aspirins dry. The woman Jeff had pointed out to her is there. A reed-slim, very attractive woman who looks to be in her late fifties. She's peering into a mirror, applying lip gloss.

"Hello. You came with Jeff, didn't you? He was always my favorite in the family." She smiles warmly at Terry. "I'm his Aunt Lindsay."

"The children's book editor?"

"Right! I, um, noticed the aspirins. Are you feeling a little under the weather?"

59

"A little."

One of Terry's current resolutions is not to whine. But this woman looks so kind. So calm. There's an air of inner confidence about her that is immensely attractive. As she sews on the button, sitting on the end of Jeff's parents' bed in her slip, Terry finds herself telling Lindsay about her sleepless night, about her mother's acid comment delivered earlier that afternoon after she arrived to baby-sit.

"I'm standing there in my son's room, Lindsay, surrounded by a vaporizer, a jug of lemon and honey, and the prescription drug the doctor recommended for him. Then my mother walks in and says, 'Well, what can you expect? He's a neglected child from a broken home now. I'm not surprised the poor little thing's sick.'"

"Life is difficult. I find it really helps if I just take it One Day at a Time," Lindsay says.

Terry stares at her. One Day at a Time. Such a typically *"program"* thing to say.

Lindsay is opening her purse. *"I've found this helps with the rough days too,"* she says. *"I repeat it whenever I feel stressed."*

Terry looks down and sees that Lindsay has given her a copy of the Serenity Prayer. She must be a recovering alcoholic. Cautiously, she tries out the sentence that anyone in the program recognizes. *"Are you,"* she asks, *"a friend of Bill W.'s?"*

"I certainly am. For almost ten years."

"But Jeff said that no one in his family was alcoholic. . . ."

"I don't think he knows, Terry. He was away at the university, in Oregon, the year I hit bottom."

The relief Terry feels at being able to talk about Jeff to someone who understands is almost overwhelming.

"I've been feeling terrible because he seems to think there's something shameful about being a recovering alcoholic," she explains to Lindsay. *"I've tried to make him understand that it's a disease. That none of us had a choice. . . ."*

"He's buying into the stigma. He's not exactly alone in that, is he?" Lindsay asks. She chuckles, and gives Terry a hug. The feathers of her hat, smelling faintly of jasmine, brush against Terry's cheek. *"The main thing,"* she says, *"is that we don't buy into it."*

✳ ✳ ✳

*At the same time we say through our lips that alcohol-
ism is a chronic disease, many of us feel in our guts that it
is a moral or self-inflicted problem.*
— DR. LeCLAIR BISSELL,
A recovering alcoholic
and physician

*One evening, I was putting on my coat in the hall-
way, when my mother asked me where I was going. I told
her I was going to AA meeting. "Oh," she said, "You
don't need to go there." I told her that, yes, I did. As I was
closing the front door behind me, she called out, "Well,
don't ride with any of those alcoholics, will you?"*
— JOYCE, sixty

✳ ✳ ✳

One of the hardest things for people who don't understand
alcoholism to do is to separate the disease from the person.
And the stigma attached to alcoholism can be a very slippery
place for us in recovery. Because it's so prevalent — because
so many people feel there's something "not very nice" about
us — it's easy to believe it ourselves!

The first party I went to in sobriety was an anniversary
party for a married couple who were both recovering alcoholics. My friend Tom took me as his date.

"Just about everybody there will be a recovering alcoholic," he told me.

As we approached the area, I saw that it was a very exclusive neighborhood. Tall gates. High walls. Masses of trees.
My first reaction was one of surprise that a party of alcoholics
should be held in such a nice neighborhood! I knew that Tom
was in the country club, but I thought he was an exception,
and that most alcoholics would be "down and out" because
we had all thrown so much away.

I was still thinking in stereotypes.

About a week later, a friend asked me to go with her to a
meeting of Overeaters Anonymous. I probably weighed

around 110 that night. I was only just beginning to lose the gaunt, hollow-cheeked appearance I'd had when I hit bottom. But everyone was very friendly. Nobody said, "My God, what are *you* doing here?"

I sat there all evening listening to stories of compulsive eating, of desperate bingeing. One woman described how she got up in the middle of the night and ate a whole jar of mayonnaise. With her fingers!

I felt disgusted. *What sickening behavior!* I thought. *Surely, she could have controlled herself better than that?*

Then I realized that no, she couldn't. She had been addicted to eating, just as I had been to drinking. But if I, a recovering addict myself, was sitting there condemning her, how easy it must be for society in general to feel prejudice. To condemn *me* as an alcoholic woman.

* * *

The stigma's much worse if you're a woman. My ex-husband is a raving alcoholic, and has been for years. But to this day his friends regard him as a Richard Burton type. They think of him as a "good 'ole boy."
— ANDREA, forty-two

I think the stigma's even worse for a woman who lives in one of those small towns where everybody knows everybody. I met a woman named Rose who told me she was always the only woman at the AA meetings in her small town in Michigan. I really admire her. That must have taken guts for her to walk in and say, "I'm an alcoholic."
— JOYCE, sixty

* * *

All of the recovering women who shared their stories for this book said that they felt the stigma was much harsher for women.

The phrase "to drink like a man" means to drink a lot and hold it well. When I was growing up, in Southwestern and Southern states, it was impressed on me that men could hold their liquor. Men could drink all night. Men could have a wonderful time and drink you under the table.

Today the phrase "to drink like a lady" still implies drinking lightly and getting home in time to make dinner for the family. One glass of sherry or one glass of white wine before dinner always seemed "sissy" to me. It represented all the submissive women I had known, the women I didn't want to be like.

Why do so many people feel more disgust when a woman gets drunk? The roots are deep-seated. They have their base in the role of women in society. Morally, women are expected to uphold hearth and home. Nobody wants to think of their mother, their wife, or their daughter in a smoky bar, mascara smeared, skirt hiked, sliding drunkenly off a stool and onto the floor.

I can remember being aware of the stigma very early, when I was about eleven. By this time, my father was an attorney for the Atomic Energy Commission, so we were upper middle-class. We used to go to these huge social barbecues at someone's home where all the men gathered outdoors around an enormous stone barbecue. They'd barbecue beef and fish and even have lobsters boiling on the top.

And all the men would be out there drinking with their feet up on the benches of the picnic tables. Laughing. Joking. Having fun. (To me it always looked as though they were having a wonderful time.)

And where were the women?

They were in the kitchen making potato salad. Unpacking things. Carrying things — like beasts of burden — from the kitchen to the barbecue. Back and forth. "Hey, Helen, there's no salt." Back and forth.

As a child, I felt that going from the women's area to the men's was, literally, like passing from one physical area to another. I envied the men. The things they did seemed to have value. From what I heard of their conversations, they were running the world.

The things the women were doing — cooking and cleaning up — seemed to be more like punishments!

And the women, I noticed, drank in secret. Not all of them, of course. Some were drinking openly. But some were "sneaking" more drinks than was apparently acceptable.

One of them, a woman named Eileen, left a vivid memory with me.

Eileen was the wife of a prominent car dealer in town. A good 'ole boy. She had a beautiful house. Financially, she had everything she could possibly want. On the afternoon I remember, I was helping Eileen in the kitchen. Sounds of laughter from the men outside drifted in through the window. Eileen poured herself a shot glass of bourbon, and, just as she was raising it to her mouth, her child walked in the kitchen door. And she *ducked* down behind the kitchen counter!

Even at the age of eleven that seemed to me to be such a humiliating position for a woman. Eileen, poor Eileen, had everything she could possibly want in material things, but no self-respect. It left a vivid impression on me.

As I grew older, drinking became, like everything else in my life, a competitive activity. I didn't want to be a submissive "traditional" woman like my mother. She'd had a terrible life. I wanted to do things of value, like the men.

Women, I reasoned, could have any career they wanted if they were given the opportunity. And, probably subconsciously, I also reasoned that a woman could drink like a man. I went to great lengths to prove this, ignoring my own physiology and psychology in the process.

I think that, like so many women, I was playing a "catch up" game with the men.

* * *

Being a female drinker seemed to make me one of the boys, and I don't see that parallel with men in any way. Male drinkers don't become one of the gals! Being a female drinker made me more desirable to men in some ways, but in the important ways, I lost. . . . Men still seem to want a woman they can take home to Mama!

— SHON, twenty-eight
A former cocktail waitress
at a popular disco

✳ ✳ ✳

Society's view of women who drink heavily really hasn't changed much since I was eleven. Morally, women are still supposed to uphold hearth and home.

As recovering alcoholics, we are working a program that requires sobriety, honesty, and integrity. For us, these qualities mean our survival! But to admit to someone that you are a recovering alcoholic is often to see, in their eyes, that their image of you has been tarnished. It should be the opposite.

✳ ✳ ✳

I think that since I respect myself today and take great pride in the achievements that I've accomplished, others can't help but respect me also.

— SHON, twenty-eight
In recovery for one year

✳ ✳ ✳

I feel the same way that Shon does. In sobriety, our lives speak for themselves. Almost every recovering woman I've met has possessed a remarkable core of inner strength.

In recovery, we are all morally responsible for our behavior. What we're *not* responsible for is accepting a larger blame from society, the one that says, "You are a bad woman."

You're not. Perhaps in the days when you were mind-altered by this disease, you did a few crazy things (perhaps, like me, you did a lot of them), but now you no longer have to carry this huge burden.

But isn't society's view of us changing now? Isn't it softening? What about the sympathy well-respected women in the public eye have generated when they've admitted to alcoholism? And what about all those glossy magazine covers splashed with headlines about celebrity recovery?

Surely people understand more about addiction now than at any time in history?

Well yes, on the surface they do.

In society's view, one of the worst things a woman can be is promiscuous.

And that's the stereotype of an alcoholic woman.

But those stereotypes I mentioned earlier — the bag lady shuffling down an alley, a bottle of cheap wine clinking in her shopping cart, or the hollow-eyed wreck, wrapped in a sleazy housecoat, who is waiting for the liquor store to open at 8:00 A.M. — still linger. A *reality* of life today is that many alcoholic women reach their lowest point while they still have a successful career.

Jan, who has a high-paying job in public relations, is a good example of an alcoholic woman of today, a woman who has never slept in doorways.

In her late forties now, Jan was divorced when she had five young children. Within a year, her ex-husband had begun another family with his second wife, so Jan had to support her children almost single-handedly. She remembers:

> *I began drinking late — when I was thirty. I was slender when I began drinking, a size six. By the time I was forty, I weighed 197 pounds, but I thought I was still gorgeous. I was up to a quart of scotch a day.*
>
> *One night I was in a bar, dancing on top of the juke box, and the bartender yelled, "Hey, get down off there.*

*You'll break it!" I yelled back, "No! I'm having a good
time!" He threw me out.*

*That was my first moment of clarity. It was raining,
and I was sitting in the street, on the curb, thinking* I've
been thrown out of a bar! Me! This sort of thing
doesn't happen to people like me!

*I realized then that I'd hit the point where I was a
drunk. My children had been telling me that for the past
two years, but it hadn't had any effect. I'd been deluding
myself because I still had my career. That night I got to a
phone and called AA.*

In recovery, when, like Jan, we look back at the things we
did when we were drinking, our feelings of shame can carry
over, making shame a slippery place for us. In society's view,
one of the worst things a woman can be is promiscuous. And
that's the most popular stereotype of an alcoholic woman.

Many of us, however, did none of these things.

The following story is one I heard a woman tell at a meeting, after another woman had just shared a story about life in
the alcoholic "fast lane."

*You gals who went out to the bars and drank, and had
fun, that wasn't my life. I drank behind my ironing board.*

*I would sit in front of the TV and I would drink, and
iron, drink, and iron. And I pictured all the excitement in
the lives of gals like you. And I would wonder why I
couldn't be out there having a good time.*

*Eventually in recovery, I came to realize that it was
all the same. The girls in the bars weren't having any
more fun than I was!*

We realize a lot of things in recovery.

One of the reasons many of us are willing to accept
society's devalued image of us is that we feel so guilty. . . .

We're so good at feeling guilty!
We say, I feel guilty —

- because I lied to you.
- because I concealed my feelings from you.
- because I wasn't a perfect mother.
- because my drinking damaged my children.

And the woman who drinks behind an ironing board feels just as much guilt as the woman who wakes up in bed with a stranger.

One of my favorite "guilt" stories goes back to the years of my second marriage. We were living in Wisconsin then, and we gave wonderful dinner parties. Like everything else in my life, I was very competitive about these parties.

One crisp fall day, I sent my children out to pick maple leaves.

"Pick only the most beautiful ones," I told them. "The ones with the most color."

Then, perfectionist that I was, I ironed these beautiful maple leaves between sheets of waxed paper, wrote the menu for the evening on the back (a very complex process), and placed one on each guest's dinner plate.

There were twelve guests that night.

I'll serve the pumpkin soup in twelve little scooped-out pumpkins, I thought. *It'll stun them.*

It took hours. All that seed scooping! I even scooped out a huge pumpkin to use as a tureen. And, of course, being such a good mother, and so thrifty, in the middle of cooking for twelve guests, I roasted all those seeds and made healthy snacks for the children.

That evening, as I ladled out the soup from my huge, scooped-out pumpkin, the guests murmured "Ooo . . ." and "Ahhh . . ." In less than a minute, the pumpkin soup had disappeared.

I was still standing there with the ladle in my hand. I was stunned at how quickly this phenomenal achievement of mine was over. There was nothing left to do but clear away all those hollow little pumpkins and bring on the next course. By the middle of dinner, I was drinking heavily, feeling that my accomplishments weren't appreciated — that my guests were second-rate. These people just didn't seem to realize how much effort I had put in!

The question, "But who asked you to scoop out thirteen pumpkins?" didn't occur to me.

I had little insight that my dinner was created, not out of love, not out of wanting to do something nice for others, but out of that ageless and timeless Superwoman syndrome.

I felt that

Just Being "Me" Wasn't Enough

This combination of unrealistic standards, incredible perfectionism, and the unreasonable demands many of us make on ourselves creates a no-win situation. It feeds our alcoholism when we drink in response to stress.

Our incredible shame comes from the fact that we didn't measure up to our own unrealistic standards.

We couldn't!

* * *

The stigma of alcoholism is the reason many families cover up for a woman who drinks. Or they may ignore the problem — perhaps hoping it will go away. Pam, who is in her early forties and has been in recovery for five years, tells the following story:

> *When I was at the stage where I was waking up every two hours during the night and drinking vodka — my body couldn't go without alcohol for longer than that — my in-laws came for a visit.*
>
> *No one mentioned my drinking. I kept going. I cooked for everyone. I cleaned the house. I shopped. My*

liver was in such bad shape that while I was driving them around sightseeing, I was often bent over double.

"I've got cramps," I used to tell them. Neither of them said anything, but years later, when I was about four years into recovery, my mother-in-law said, "Dad and I thought you were drinking yourself to death." It astonished me that at the time, they never said anything to me.

No one would think of asking someone dying of one of the "respectable" diseases to run a house, hold down a job, and take care of the needs of a husband and family. We just don't ask severely debilitated people to perform these functions. But we ask it of alcoholic women who are often very sick, detoxifying, and on an emotional roller coaster.

It's often hard for women to recover from alcoholism *because* of this dual-jeopardy — the double burden of being alcoholic and also being stigmatized.

But . . . SO WHAT?

This stigma is society's problem, not ours. Even though society sees us this way, we still have to recover. WE still have to "get real."

Developing a closely knit support group of other recovering women, which Terry has begun to do in beginning a friendship with Lindsay, is extremely important in overcoming the stigma, the shame, and the guilt.

In recovery, those of us who have always felt competitive or that we were "not enough," make the exciting discovery that we don't have to justify ourselves by what we *do*.

Who We Are Is Enough

I always felt I didn't have a right to take up space on this earth.

— CAT, twenty-seven

* * *

We don't have to apologize for the space we take up by losing weight. We don't have to apologize if we work at home and don't have a salaried job. And, if we do have an outside job, we don't have to half-kill ourselves by being a slave to housework on the weekends because we feel so guilty.

Not all of us have bizarre, promiscuous sexual histories. Yet, obviously, alcohol changes our experiences. Alcohol works on the centers of the brain that affect our caution, our moral judgment, and our reasoning.

Perhaps unlike the woman who drank behind her ironing board, you *were* "one of the gals in the bar." Perhaps your past history involved promiscuity? Infidelity? Betrayal? Perhaps, like me, you violated your own value system?

How do you manage not to feel guilty? Not to feel ashamed?

In recovery, it's critically important to face up to all those remembered situations with program solutions. A sponsor can help with a Fourth and Fifth Step. We do this in order to accept the past, to put it behind us.

And Move On

In a program of recovery, we have all the resources we need to cope with any challenges that crop up. We have the tools of the program. We have the respect and the support of others who are recovering too. We have wonderful role models of other women who talk openly about their recovery. Women who will help us in any way they can.

Everything Is There for Us If We Want It

In recovery, we are truly transformed. As sober women, we hold our heads high. We don't need to apologize or explain ourselves. Today, I know that the word *lady* applies to me. I know it applies to you too.

CHAPTER FIVE

Sparkling Women
with Clean Hair!
Our Role Models

*I thought it was really funny that Mary Tyler Moore
was a recovering alcoholic. I used to watch that series on
TV when she and Dick Van Dyke were the perfect couple.
I thought she was terrific. Then she became a career
woman on the next series, and I thought, We're just
alike! I secretly believed that. Well, we are. Now we're
both recovering alcoholics. I still admire her and think
she's a great role model.*

— RICKY, fifty-one
A free-lance writer

* * *

In the kitchen of the house in New Mexico, my father's
girlfriend Helen and I are staring at three loaves of bread on
the kitchen table. They look like three adobe blocks.

"I'm sure they don't look anything like the ones your
mother used to bake, do they?" Helen asks me. She's smiling.
Her eyes look bright with amusement.

"Well, not much, Helen," I admit. My Southern mother,
before she became very ill, had been a wonderful cook.

I peer at the loaves anxiously. They look terrible! And this is the second batch she's made. The first lot are in the trash. I feel very nervous for Helen. My father made such a big point, when he handed her my mother's recipe for this complicated yeast bread, about how much he enjoyed it. What if he loses his temper? With my father you can never tell. I've seen him explode into fury over a piece of burnt toast.

I would have been terrified if I'd tried to make bread for him, and it had turned out like this.

"Perhaps it would be more merciful to cover these poor little loaves up. Give them a decent burial," Helen murmurs. I watch as she whisks a white tablecloth from one of the cupboard drawers. In her sleeveless blue linen sheath dress — completely inappropriate for cooking — she looks as smart as a magazine advertisement. This thirty-eight-year-old nursing supervisor, so full of joy and humor, so comfortable with herself, seems beautiful to me.

I'm sixteen years old, and I love Helen. I want to be just like her.

She's the first independent career woman I've been close to. She lives alone — my idea of Heaven — in a glamorous apartment. She has white furniture. There are huge, glossy art books piled on her coffee table. In our dark, cheerless house, my father would never have allowed me to spend money for something as impractical as a coffee-table art book.

Outside, in the driveway, a car door slams.

"Oh, that must be your father," Helen says cheerfully.

I can feel my heart beating. So fast. Thud-thud. Thud-thud. If he flies into one of his unreasonable rages, will it drive Helen away? In the two months she's been dating my father, she's been the best thing that has ever happened to our family.

Certainly she's the best thing that's ever happened to me. Before Helen came, my father had always insisted that one whole day of the weekend be spent doing the heavy cleaning. The other day had to be spent studying. The lives of my school friends seemed so free in comparison to mine.

But now, Helen simply tells my father, "Oh, Ann Ruth and I are going clothes shopping." Or "Ann Ruth and I are going to the museum." And away we go in her red convertible. She even trusts me to drive her red convertible!

I hear the sound of the front door opening.

Thud-thud. Thud-thud.

Helen has covered up the loaves. They sit mutely, three bumps under a white tablecloth. A panicky feeling overwhelms me. My father is in the hallway. He's opening the kitchen door. . . .

"We've a surprise for you, honey!" Helen tells him. Like a conjuror's assistant, she whisks off the cloth.

My father stares at the bread.

"Do you think they might look a little better if we glazed them with something?" Helen asks him. "Varnish, maybe?"

And my father is *laughing!* He has his arm around Helen's shoulders, and he's staring down at those ridiculous loaves and laughing. Helen is laughing. I'm laughing.

In our house! No one ever laughs in our house.

And my hopes begin to bloom. Maybe they'll get married! For once, maybe, my father won't ruin everything, and we'll be able to keep Helen in our family.

* * *

A few months later, Helen told me she was leaving. She had accepted a transfer to another hospital, in Texas.

She loved my father, she told me. She loved all of us, especially me. In fact, if my father had asked her to marry him a few months ago, she would have done so. But the more she had seen of his temper, his drinking, and his brutal treatment of his sons (by that time he considered me too big to hit in front of other people), the more she had come to realize that it would never work.

I can remember that afternoon so clearly. We were in her apartment, drinking iced tea, and she'd just given me a beautiful set of white luggage for graduating from high school at sixteen.

I remember the apartment blurring around me.

I was so *angry!*

Not with Helen. I could hardly blame her for not wanting to take on my father and his three abused children. But the fury I felt toward my father is indescribable. He'd ruined everything. Again! The same thought kept running through my mind, over and over and over. I thought, *First he killed my mother. And now he's driven Helen away.*

I seethed with anger. I *burned* with it.

* * *

My role model was Barbara Stanwyck. You know that movie she made — the one where she was the glamorous boss of a gang of outlaws? Well, I wanted to be Barbara Stanwyck, and go live with a gang of outlaws in a hole-in-the-wall. And all the gang would protect me.

— SANDRA, forty-seven

* * *

I grew up with fantasy role models too. Dale Evans. Nancy Drew. Scarlett O'Hara. But Helen, if she'd stayed around, would have been a wonderful real life role model for me.

Girls who grew up in the fifties rarely had a real role model of an independent woman who could choose her own lifestyle. We didn't know of any Geraldine Ferraros or Barbara Jordans then. Just as Barbara Stanwyck in her role as a bandit queen appealed to Sandra, most of our role models were a hodge-podge of people from the movies, or characters from fiction.

But women of any era — the fifties or today — may have learned roles that don't work, roles that contribute to addiction.

* * *

> *I never really looked up to any woman. Maybe it sounds silly, but there were some cartoon characters I really wanted to be like. They were women with super-natural powers as well as beauty. I think that's what I wanted. To be able to pick and choose — men, places, things — to have complete control. To be my own, and everyone else's higher power.*
>
> — BARBARA, twenty
> A part-time student and
> recovering addict who
> lives at home with her
> divorced mother

❊   ❊   ❊

Melanie, who is twenty-seven, is a recovering alcoholic and addict with nearly three years sobriety. She works in the media as a technical engineer, one of few women in this male-dominated field. Melanie says:

> *There's a song by Willie Nelson, "My heroes have always been cowboys. . . ." I can remember lots of men I admired. War leaders like Patton. Cowboys like Clint Eastwood and John Wayne. All men who swaggered and bullied to get their own way. I liked Frank Sinatra singing "My Way."*
> *Now I'm in a very frustrating career — I have to fight for everything that is routinely given to the guys I work with. And if I earn compliments or a bonus for a good job, the guys laugh and say, "It's because you're a woman!" I can't win. My role models aren't much help today.*

Melanie's role models were related to her drinking and using. One of the ways she tried to fit in at work was to go out drinking and using with the men.

I'd elbow my way into a group that was going out after work. Most of them would have a few drinks and leave. Pretty soon, I was staying too long, getting into some embarrassing situations, having hangovers.

Later, I was dealing drugs. Well, not exactly dealing. I was giving drugs away in order to be "one of the guys." It didn't work! Now, that's a problem, too, because I have to overcome the old image. I guess that's what we call "wreckage of the past."

But when I think about what I've learned, I'm overwhelmed with gratitude. I know I've got a great second chance, and — excuse the pun — I'm not blowing it!

* * *

I didn't have a role model for my alcoholism. I did it all by myself.

— SHEILA, fifty-one

* * *

I've often pointed out in my writing and speaking that young women don't have any role models for drinking behavior. It's almost unknown for anyone's mother to give her lessons on how to drink, or instruction on how to recognize the symptoms of dependency.

Do you know any woman who sat down on the end of her daughter's bed — on a quiet evening, perhaps, when they had the house to themselves — and said something like, "Shelly — it's time we had a little talk, dear. Let me explain the progression of alcoholism to you"?

Yet, inevitably, a certain percentage of girls will become alcoholics and other addicts, codependents, and overeaters, or experience a combination of problems. The list goes on!

* * *

> *I used to think I was the only person who drank as I did. I'd be watching TV talk shows and I'd think,* How can they talk in public . . . be so articulate . . . without having a drink first?
>
> — Joyce, sixty

* * *

While we are drinking, who do we use as role models? Who do we talk to about our hangovers, and our blackouts, and our feelings of isolation? Our friends are not likely to be alcoholic women who have successfully managed to get sober. Alcoholic women *conceal* themselves. Again, that's the old theme of "looking good." All our energy goes into looking good. So until we become so dysfunctional that we're forced to recognize it — by the time we're *open* to the idea that other women could be alcoholic — we're too isolated by our illness to look around and find any. By then, we're just surviving behind a wall of denial.

Young girls in dysfunctional families often start drinking at a very early age. I drank in school. I drank when, after my early high school graduation, I ran away to Kentucky to attend college and live with my mother's sister (another alcoholic who, true to the drama of alcoholic families, hated my father and fanned the flames of anger I felt toward him). I drank as a young wife and mother. I drank while I was earning two master's degrees, and a Ph.D.

And in all those years, apart from the brief time with Helen, women were not important to me. My mother, whom I both pitied and resented, died when I was thirteen. My relatives, including the aunt I lived with, were all alcoholic. There wasn't a healthy, sober role model in my life.

I did have women friends. One of them was my childhood friend Elizabeth. Elizabeth drank like I did. We kept in touch over the years. By the time I had reached the "geographical escape" stage of my disease, she and her husband had moved to a small town in Southern California, very close to the Mexican border.

"We're opening a restaurant called The Wild Turkey," she wrote. "Come and see us."

Suddenly, everything seemed clear to me. It was the pressures of my fast-paced career that were driving me to drink too much. What I needed was a simpler life. Yes, that was it! I'd give up my career, give up my degrees, and become a waitress at The Wild Turkey, and all would be well.

I moved in with Elizabeth and her husband, a man who drank vodka around the clock. All three of us drank beer. Whoever was up first in the morning brought the other two beer in bed. My body was by then so addicted to alcohol that I used to carry a can of beer into the shower with me. I didn't really think anything of it, except that it was a nuisance to have watery beer.

Both my career as a waitress and the restaurant were short-lived. I had begun to use cocaine. Like The Wild Turkey, I was headed for the end.

Elizabeth and I had been friends nearly all our lives. Our families had lived across the street from each other, and as babies we often shared the same playpen. But our friendship deteriorated as we, ourselves, deteriorated. Each day, as we began drinking, our self-centered fears surfaced. When we drank together we both got into the same anger, paranoia, and jealousy.

Our friendship didn't survive.

❋ ❋ ❋

I always liked the way most bars are dim, shadowy. I would go into bars dressed in a suit, carrying a briefcase — because that way I looked like I was somebody — and it was an ego thing for me to see just how many men came on to me. The more guys who wanted to buy me a drink the better I felt. I felt comfortable in bars. Going to the beach scared me. The beach was so bright and full of

*women who looked better in a swimsuit than I did. I
always saw other women as my rivals, as competition.*
— CAT, twenty-seven

* * *

By the time I got into a program of recovery I had no close
women friends. I had become such a liar to conceal my habit
that, as a friend, I couldn't be counted on.

I really wasn't enthusiastic about women in general anyway. They had never been much help to me. When I was a
child, they were always leaving me. As I grew older, I began
seeing them, as many women do, as my competition.

It was *men*, I believed, who had all the answers to life. Men
had the best jobs, the power. Men could help you to get ahead.
They were buddies. They were desirable.

Men could also be controlled. With flirtation, with seduction and flattery, they were easily fooled. Or at least they
appeared to be.

So, when I began the process of recovery and going to
Twelve Step meetings, I looked to men to guide me, to give me
answers. I began to think that maybe another husband was
"the answer" — someone supportive, who would take care of
me. (Although neither of my two ex-husbands had taken care
of me.) I was looking for someone — anyone — who could
help to take away some of the terrible pain I was in.

And what I found instead were all these women who were
like Helen, living successfully. Some had men in their lives,
some didn't. They were women who were living successfully,
sober first, and then they were women who were successfully
alive.

They had a strength I wanted.

A simple truth can hit you when you finally get sober. I
thought, *Oh, wow! There are lots of women in the world who are
like Helen!*

I shared my ugly, ugly secrets, and they shared with me.
For the first time in my life, I didn't have to keep up a false

pretense of looking good on the outside, while secretly falling apart on the inside. The love I received from these women was unconditional.

And I began to realize that these women could teach me how to stay sober. This didn't happen to me overnight, though. It took a while for the fog to lift.

* * *

I married two alcoholics, because they asked me.
— GLORIA, thirty-seven

* * *

I dated men I met in my first thirty days of sobriety — even though, in the Twelve Step program I follow, there's a generally understood prohibition against it. I was such a people pleaser, it was almost impossible for me to say no. I went out with everyone who asked me. I believe that, on some subconscious level, I was seeing every man as my father, and God only knew what the consequences would be if I wasn't obedient.

I remember one terrible date. I'll call him Howard.

In his dark and grimy little house, Howard made us a meal of rubbery sausage patties, fried potatoes, and Pepsi served in jelly glasses. The house had a strange smell, a mingling of mildewed shag carpet and the dozens of opened cat-food tins that were sitting around.

After dinner, Howard pressed me back on a balding brown velvet sofa, and reached across me to turn off the lights. The TV was on, and in its flickering glow I could see that he was leering.

"I've been reading . . ." he murmured.

"Ah . . ." I said.

". . . that frequent sexual orgasms are good for women in early sobriety."

My heart was pounding with panic. I told him that I had been to the dentist that morning and one of my teeth had just started to ache. It was, I explained, a really agonizing toothache. So, really, I had better go home. Even though he had been so kind about having me over to dinner, and the sausage patties had been delicious, I would have to leave.

"That's too bad," he muttered, staring at my legs. He was still leering. "How about next Friday?"

That was on a Sunday.

I spent the next four days worrying about Howard. How was I going to get out of dating him again? The message still lingering — over all the years! — from my domineering father was that you did what a man wanted. And this very old tape about dating was still playing inside my head.

Fortunately, that same week I found my sponsor. The night I met her, I was wearing a drab navy blue suit. In those first weeks of recovery, life can be so scary. I wore navy blue to "fit in" to recovery, to be unobtrusive. My mother's advice from all those years ago — about the ladylike qualities of navy blue still echoed in my head. I was terrified of attracting unnecessary attention to myself, of being thought cheap.

So, there I was in new sobriety at a meeting, buttoned up tightly in my navy blue suit, feeling like a nothing person. And there was a woman speaking at the podium in a beautiful silk dress wildly printed with all the jewel colors — amethyst, emerald green, sapphire blue. As I listened, I knew the colors she was wearing reflected how she felt about life.

She glowed!

I looked at her and thought, *Well, I'm never going to be like* her.

Then she began to talk about how addicted she had been. How trapped. She began telling her story? It was mine! And inside my head something clicked. I thought, *That was me!* In that instant, I could relate to her and feel a bond with her. At the end of the meeting, I approached this incredible woman and asked her if she would be my sponsor.

I asked her what she thought I could do about Howard.

"Ann, it's very simple," she said. "You have choices. You can call him up and tell him you don't want to date him. Or *I* can call him up and tell him you don't want to date him. . . ."

The truth hit me suddenly. I hadn't *chosen* Howard. I didn't find him at all attractive. I had accepted him simply because he'd asked me.

This insight said, *Now that I'm sober, I can choose who I date, and who I spend time with. I'm no longer doing things because I feel guilty, because I feel remorse.*

Then, just as Terry had felt after the breakup of her bad marriage, it struck me, that feeling of "Well, what do *I* want?"

And I realized that I didn't really know.

I also realized that I was very confused about men, and this became part of my decision to remain celibate for the rest of my first year of sobriety. I did go out on occasional dates, but they were for practice. I said good-night on my doorstep.

No newly recovering alcoholic, male or female, has a good sense of self. How could we? We have been living a life of deceit and fraud. And while we are discovering who we really are, we are not ready for a committed sexual relationship.

Not all women feel about this as I do. There are women who will say, "I met my husband in my first month of sobriety — and we've been happily married for twenty years."

There are women who say that they *needed* to feel loved and desired in early sobriety. They dated men they met at recovery group meetings, and they insist that no one pressured them for sex, or "Thirteenth-Stepped" them. (Thirteenth-Stepping happens when someone, male or female, comes on, sexually, to a newcomer.)

Cat, who began drinking in the fourth grade, and who was only twenty-four when she hit bottom three years ago, tells the following story:

> I was so scared at my first AA group meeting. I was terrified that somebody would ask me to speak. So I sat under a table, at the back of the room, and drew my knees

up. I stayed there all through the meeting, coming out just in time to pick up a guy who was there.

I just kind of grabbed on to this guy's shirttails and said, "Please don't leave me. I'll do anything you want."

He had two years of sobriety, but he was out of work. He moved in with me, and for the first 100 days of my sobriety, I supported him and my five-year-old son. I had been fired from my job with a computer company, and I was working in a high-stress job in telephone solicitations.

I couldn't sleep. I used to spend the nights pacing or sitting in a rocking chair and crying. He would get up and comfort me. I was in a twilight zone where everything seemed unreal for about six months. All that crystal I had snorted. I felt it was six months before the drugs left my body. It was six months of chaos and confusion.

My belief is that you are being unfair to *yourself* if you don't take your relationships in recovery in nice, slow, easy steps. In a way, you are re-creating the steps of childhood development, the steps that, for most of us, were flawed in some way.

In sobriety we need to grow up all over again.

If you follow the theme that in sobriety we come in as babies, and grow up through the teenage ranks, the first person you need to have a relationship with is a mother. You need to be nurtured and loved. That mother is the AA meeting or a sponsor. We need to experience unconditional love.

The natural chronology of life is like that. First you are friends with

Your Mother

Then you are friends with

Your Father
Your Puppy, Your Toys, Your Dolls

Then you are friends with

Your Girlfriends

that adolescent period of being a giggly girl.
Then, as you learn who you are, as you build self-esteem

You Start to Form Relationships with Men

* * *

When I was nine months sober, my children gave me a golden cocker spaniel puppy for my birthday. I still have Gatsby. He was my sanity. My Twelve Step program saved my life, and Gatsby, who adores me unconditionally, saved my sanity. In new sobriety, he made my life less lonely. I started waking up with his little blond head on my pillow instead of making some very bad mistakes. (Passion on the brown velvet sofa with Howard, the cat-tin man, would, I feel, certainly have been a mistake.)

This transition period of new sobriety, while both our minds and bodies are healing, is kind of a "holding action."

And it is while we are in this transition stage that it's important for us to find role models. Women who are strong at their core, who will accept us just as we are and reassure us that it's okay not to date or to plunge ahead. And — in the case of Thirteenth-Stepping — they will be there for us as knowledgeable guides. (A guide who will not abandon us if we ignore the guidance!) Married women, or women in committed relationships, need an experienced sponsor and other sober women, to show them how to build and improve the relationships that they have.

I'm not suggesting that celibacy in the first year is the right choice for everyone. But it worked for me. It's a choice that I'm glad I made.

Another choice that I'm glad I made was to accept the friendship of a woman named Yvonne. Because her sobriety date was so close to mine, I discovered that we could talk about all the embarrassing, humiliating, petty details of sober living. I could trust Yvonne. She didn't laugh at me because she was where I was.

A relationship with a sponsor is for guidance. You talk to her about the important things. But with your same-length buddy you can talk about the silly things you don't want to burden your sponsor with. I always thought of Yvonne as my "Silly-Buddy."

I could say to her, "Gosh, I was sitting in my car at a red light today, and I felt like I was going to die from anxiety." And she would say something like, "I know! I've felt exactly the same way."

What she didn't say was, "Oh, don't be silly!"

While You Are Building Self-Esteem You Need to Surround Yourself with These Women

In my new sobriety, when I began going to meetings, I heard over and over "Ask for help." I had a lot of trouble, at first, with asking for help. Around the time I began going to meetings, there was a trash bag commercial on TV. It was one in which a little voice cried Wimpy! Wimpy! Wimpy! And that was exactly how I felt.

I used to sit through meetings feeling terrible, but it seemed weak to admit it. I felt I should somehow be able to "tough it out."

Little Ann, the child in braids who once lugged laundry through an Arizona trailer park, was still inside me. Wasn't she the "responsible" one? The one who could handle anything? Of course she was. She had been taught that from her earliest childhood.

When someone in a meeting gave me a list of phone numbers and suggested I call them, I didn't really want to. I saw it as "Exercise 22" in the homework of recovery — something I *must* succeed at. Heaven forbid I should flunk recovery!

One night I sat down with my list of numbers and began dialing. I called all of them. Some women were out. Some had answering machines. But the ones I connected with invariably said something like, "Thanks for calling, Ann. I needed someone to talk to."

They *always* seemed to need someone to talk to. *This is great*, I thought. *I don't need to say anything.* And once I learned the secret to this phone calling, I was comfortable with it.

What I didn't understand, for a long time, was that it was

Connecting People to Me

They *were* giving me help. I was becoming a part of this network — woven into the fabric of it. I had made myself vulnerable without trying. And I discovered that any questions I had, I could find the answers to, somewhere in this vast network.

It's healthy for those of us who are recovering alcoholics to help each other. It helps us to stay sober. For sobriety is like love — you can't keep it unless you give it away.

* * *

My sponsor is a fantastic woman. She's my age and teaches pool exercises. Her favorite thing in the world is helping other alcoholics. She doesn't give me advice very often. She listens.

— JOYCE, sixty

I've always believed in the power of prayer. I prayed that I would find the right sponsor, and I did. Almost

*immediately. I chose a woman who has a strong spiritual-
ity, a wonderful sense of humor, and — what attracted me
to her the most — she's happy!"*

— GAIL, early forties

* * *

No one woman, however fantastic, will have all the qualities you need. In alcoholism, we tried to be all things to all
people. In sobriety, we learn that each of us has strengths in
different areas.

Terry has a warm, kind, motherly sponsor named Joanne,
who is a married woman with three teenagers. Joanne has
been very supportive of Terry, but the working world is beyond her experience and she cannot, as Lindsay can, relate to
the added pressures of a woman with a fast-track career. In
Lindsay, Terry has found a mentor who is successful in business and who understands relationships with men.

* * *

*I heard this woman talking in a meeting about being
unfaithful to her husband. I was shocked. She was very
well-dressed and obviously financially well off. I just
couldn't believe that she could be admitting these things
in public! But the more I listened, the more I realized that
I wanted to be just like her; I wanted to be honest.*

— LISA, thirty-six
A compulsive overeater

* * *

As my own role models, I look today for women who are
available to

Encourage, Not Criticize

Women who can inspire me when fear, loneliness, and indecision perch on my shoulder just waiting for me to move. Like loving mothers and sisters, these women encourage me to go out and play. To explore. To grow.

If you are a recovering woman, one of the most important things about your recovery will be

The Women Who Have Gone Before You

❋ ❋ ❋

When I was a newlywed, living in New York, my husband was assigned to write a story about Alcoholics Anonymous for a magazine. This was in 1954. I didn't know anything about AA then. Not many people did. One evening, I went with my husband to an open meeting. I was sitting there, looking around, and suddenly I realized I couldn't see any women.

— JOYCE, sixty

I used to hear them talking in AA meetings about this fabulous woman named Jeanette. She was like a patron saint or something. I heard how Jeanette had helped Millie . . . and then, when they talked about Millie, she began to sound like the saint! It went on and on. Then I realized that they were all just women helping other women. No "saints." And I wanted to be one of them.

— SALLY, fifty-nine

❋ ❋ ❋

The first women in the program remind me of the women who came West in covered wagons — someone had to get over that hill first. And the rest followed.

The women who have been in the program before you made the way just a little easier for you. They are living illustrations of successful sobriety.

You do it yourself, with their help and God's.

And then you reach back to pull another woman along.

CHAPTER SIX

Rebel Without a Clue — Relationships and Codependency

I always dated alcoholic men. If they didn't drink, they weren't interesting.

— GAIL, early forties

When I woke up with a hangover, it always helped to have a husband in bed next to me.

— GLORIA, thirty-seven

* * *

The first sip of my first manhattan of the day feels wonderful. A man at a table a few feet away is trying to flirt with me. In the gloom of this Reno bar, I can see his eyes glinting. I'm twenty-eight, and this is the day of my second wedding.

I'm happy. I'm euphoric actually, as I watch the door, waiting for Vern, my fiance, to appear and whisk me off to a wedding chapel. Slot machines jangle in the background. A woman is yelling "Go, baby! Go!"

Although I'm now a university professor, the "rebel" in me has chosen to wear a thigh-high scarlet silk mini-dress and scarlet boots. I feel beautiful. (One or two drinks always makes me feel beautiful.) *This time*, I think, *it's going to be okay.*

Everything's going to be okay! Smiling in my shadowy corner, I jiggle the ice cubes around my drink to signal the waiter for another one, and I think about Vern.

He is exactly what I want.

One of the things I've always advised my patients to do is to make a written list of the things they want. When I was twenty-five, a graduate student, divorced with two small daughters, I made a list of the things I wanted in a husband. He had to be older than me. He also had to be intelligent, successful, good-looking, and exciting.

Vern is all these things. He's a full professor at a prestigious university. He's a brilliant public speaker. (He's also an alcoholic, whose disease is several years ahead of mine, but neither of us realizes this.) We're very much in love.

We've been living together for the past year. Because I want him so much, I've created a fantasy life for him. At the end of my day's work, I feed the children an early supper and put them to bed. Then I help Vern write articles; I serve him gourmet meals by candlelight; I wear sensuous clothing. (Of course, to keep up with all this, I'm drinking and using.)

Vern, with the typical grandiosity of an alcoholic, has created a fantasy world for me too. He's the kind of man who likes to give diamonds. Once, when I was pushing a cart through a supermarket, he hired a florist to follow me and hand me a dozen yellow roses, right by the frozen food section. As I was standing there clasping them, Vern suddenly appeared, shouted, "I love you!" and waltzed me down the center aisle to the sounds of supermarket Muzak and the other customers clapping.

I glance up from my second manhattan. Vern is standing in the doorway! He's just flown in from a conference in California, and he's brought the dean of another Ivy League university with him. A wedding witness?

"Ann, darling . . . that dress!" Vern says. The dean has a startled look. Vern is smiling, bending to kiss me, whispering against my hair that he thinks I look incredible.

We spend the afternoon drinking. We have a wonderful time. Everyone in the bar knows that it's our wedding day. Everyone wants to buy us drinks. At ten minutes to six, Vern realizes that we don't have a license. The license bureau will be closing in ten minutes.

"Let's go!" he cries, seizing my hand, and also propelling the now inebriated dean out of his chair.

We grab a cab. We rush to the license bureau. The door is locked, but Vern pounds on it frantically. When an annoyed-looking clerk shows up, he turns on his charm to persuade her to give us a license. It doesn't occur to either of us to wonder *why* we are rushing or why we can't wait until the morning. Both of us relish the excitement, the drama.

At 7:00 P.M., we stand side by side in the Little Chapel of the Bridal Wreath. The minister has shadows under his eyes and looks like Walter Matthau in an electric blue suit. He seems weary, as if it's been a long day.

And, suddenly, everything doesn't seem so much fun. My alcohol haze is wearing off. I'm losing my glow.

I look around and notice that there are no fresh flowers, only plastic ones. There's no music, either. The Walter Matthau-like minister yawns as he opens his white Bible. A woman who was vacuuming the hall carpet when we arrived stands beside the sleepy-looking dean as our second witness. Everything looks so . . . bedraggled. Including us! I think, *Is this the kind of wedding I really wanted? Why am I doing this?*

* * *

I was doing it, marrying in haste while Vern was still in the mood, because I was running scared.

My drinking, by then, was beginning to cause problems. I still looked good on the outside, but I was going on drinking binges, meeting men in bars, waking up hungover and remorseful. After the last binge, I'd been terrified that my drinking was going to jeopardize my chances of marrying Vern.

What if I lost him? I wanted someone strong to share the burden. Somebody powerful to protect me from the mess I was beginning to create. I didn't want to be alone.

And Vern? What was he feeling on his wedding day?

I had no idea. We never talked about feelings. I never really considered that he *had* any. I saw him as an all-wise, all-powerful, successful father figure. A man with all the answers.

Now I know that he, too, was running scared.

* * *

I never knew anybody who talked about their feelings. You talked about the outside stuff. You never talked about what was going on inside.

— GLORIA, thirty-seven

* * *

Since I've been sober, I've never gone to a wedding without feeling a little wistful. That feeling that "things could have been different if . . ."

Relationships are extremely important to almost all of us. Among recovering women of any age, there's a common thread when it comes to our past relationships. No matter how different our experiences have been — whether we've had less traumatic and more normal marriages, or we've never been married, or we've been married more times than we care to remember — that common thread exists.

That common thread is our problem with alcoholism.

The characteristics of alcoholics usually include *dependency on others to meet a great many of their needs.*

We needed others to

- keep the secret and provide protection.
- complete us, to build our flagging self-esteem, and tell us we were okay, when we were far from being okay.

- pick up the pieces. Someone had to cover the bounced checks. Someone had to make those awful phone calls, explaining that we were not going to be able to make it to work . . . or to our parents' anniversary party . . . or our daughter's fifth grade piano recital. Someone had to tidy up the details of life.
- generally enable our addiction.

＊　＊　＊

In the early stages of our addiction, if we marry or move in with someone, our alcoholism may not be full blown yet. Our dependency needs, however, usually are. Since we have never felt complete, we may look desperately for someone else to complete us.

We are like one of those picture puzzles in which children are asked to discover "what is wrong with this picture?" We look to others to complete the picture — the marriage picture, the financial picture, the career picture, the image picture.

Many of us have such a desperate need to complete this wonderful *image* picture — to "look good" — that we compromise our values. Marina, who is currently divorced and studying for her real estate license, was twenty-nine and married to a physician when she became sober fourteen years ago. She tells the following story of compromise.

> *For years, I'd had something to drink before we went to bed at night, and when I got rid of that alcohol, it was terrifying. I became aware of all the anger I felt toward my husband. He did this kind of undermining. For instance, when I was working at Sak's, he said, "You made another goddammed casserole? What do you think I am? I'm not going to come home and wait an hour for my dinner!"*
>
> *What I learned to do when we had sex was disassociate from myself. I think prostitutes must do this. I would take myself out of that bedroom, out of that bed. I wasn't*

even there with that man. And a man knows when it's just your body there, when there's no feeling. I went on like that for years and years. It got worse and worse, and he got more and more angry.

Toward the end of our marriage, I got really manipulative. I'd think things like, The MasterCard bills have come back. We'd better have sex.

Then, three years ago, while I was still married, I was in Sak's in New York City with my sister. We were standing at the handbag counter, and she looked at me and said, "You're nothing but a high class prostitute, Marina. That's what you've been for years. One more trip. One more piece of gold jewelry. One more outfit. When is it going to be enough that you are going to leave this man?"

I think that one statement was the thing that got me really going. She, above all the people in my life, could always make an honest assessment about me.

The compromises Marina made had to do with controlling her emotions, controlling her sexual reactions, and, all the time, the level of her anger was building . . . and building. Alcohol and pills, which became available to her while her husband was a medical student, took the edge off that anger for years.

＊　＊　＊

Marriage, for many women, appears to be part of looking good — someone loves us and has chosen us — that's often a critical component of an alcoholic life. The picture has got to look right, and then everything will be okay.

And we often do, at least in the early stages, manage to create a wonderful picture. Inside, though, we're so needy — so very needy — it's as though we are whispering silently, "Fix me, *please.*"

•

We don't just look to a partner to fill in our painful, empty feeling. Sometimes we look to religion or to work. Often we have babies, thinking that the baby, by loving us, will transform our life.

But most often, the relationship with the capital *R* for us is the romantic one. It's the one with someone we love — and this is the one that can create the most problems for us.

On that sunny afternoon, when Terry sat in Jeff's parents' garden watching his sister walking toward her singing groom, she, too, felt wistful. Her missed opportunities were like silent ghosts behind her chair. Would her life, she was wondering, ever be like that of the bride's? It was a very reasonable thing for her to wonder.

❋　❋　❋

In my second year of sobriety, I became real. I realized I was a woman of forty-four, with two teenagers, and not much money. My career wasn't very exciting. What, I thought, are my chances of attracting someone really exciting? What do I have to offer?
— CARMELA, forty-seven

❋　❋　❋

When we're drinking, we take the edge off the fear that our life may not turn out to be as wonderful as our dreams. In sobriety, it's important that we make a realistic assessment of ourselves.

At some point in her sobriety, Terry will realize that dreams are not about finding a perfect lover (is anyone perfect?), but that it's very realistic to examine the question, *Am I going to be happy in sobriety?* She will discover that dreams are not about finding someone romantic enough to write love songs to her, but that

Dreams Are About Good Feelings

Our dreams really come true when we have good feelings about ourselves. We still *have* dreams, but they're based on a realistic recognition of our own strengths and ability to make them come true.

Weddings are a symbol of *building* — two people building a life together.

If an alcoholic marries a "normal" person, that person is usually looking to build, to make plans, to set goals, and to grow. Since the alcoholic's expectations are totally different, the relationship can't work.

If you are a non-recovering alcoholic and you marry someone with some type of emotional problem or dysfunction — a closed, cold person, for example, who has difficulty with intimacy — the other person's problem may speed the decline of the relationship. Many emotional problems are progressive, not just alcoholism. Without some help, a closed person tends to become *more* so over time. It's a defensive posture. So the two unhealthy people can end up deteriorating on their own path, together but separate.

If two alcoholics marry each other, the downhill slide can happen even faster.

Two sick halves don't make a whole.

Vern and I loved each other. We stayed together for ten years, but we didn't build anything. We enabled each other to stay addicted. We lived daydream after daydream in a sand castle marriage with no substance. And as the first waves washed over our marriage — as the mood swings, and hangovers, and depressions, and angry fighting of this disease hit us — we continued to drink.

We went from dancing in the supermarket with roses to screaming at each other behind the locked bedroom door, thinking the children couldn't hear us. Our fights grew steadily worse. One horrible Sunday, I threatened him with a knife.

In any recovery program, you'll find that those of us who are married when we reach sobriety are in the minority. That silent whisper of *fix me! fix me!* puts a tremendous strain on any relationship.

Some relationships, for different reasons, do survive.

My friend Trudi, who was born, unwanted, in a cellar in Germany near the end of World War II, was still married when she reached the lowest point in her alcoholism. It was her husband, in fact, who realized she was going over the edge and put her into the hospital.

Two years later, Trudi's marriage is a very happy one. Along with her spiritual faith, and a sponsor she loves, she gives her husband much of the credit for her seeking sobriety. She says:

> I had been sexually abused and beaten, in Germany, by my step-father. He was a violent man who once poured lighter fluid on my mother, setting her on fire. Because of the incest, the childhood violence, I went through a very bad time when I was in therapy in early recovery. I reached a point where I didn't want sex at all.
>
> My husband was very kind, very patient. "Let's just snuggle up on the bed and I'll read you a bedtime story," he said. And that's what he did, night after night. And I was so touched by this, by the love in it. When I was a child, no one ever read me bedtime stories.

Some husbands are not this patient! The following story is one Connie, now seventy-two, shared of an experience that happened to her ten years ago when she was in early sobriety.

> I went to Hawaii with my husband when I was three weeks sober. Drinking had always been a way of life for us. So my husband had decided — because he had lost his drinking partner — that he couldn't walk anymore. There was nothing medically wrong with him!
>
> Well, I pushed him through the airport in a wheelchair — he weighed 250 pounds — and I pushed him into

the bar and then sat outside. I'd brought the Big Book * to read on the plane, but I didn't want anyone to know I was reading that book, so I had it covered with the dust jacket from Valley of the Dolls.

Oh, it was a marvelous trip. Every night my husband would have a few drinks before dinner, and then a few more, and I'd sit and watch him. I got so hungry! I didn't know you got hungry!

We were in Hawaii for two weeks, and I just kept reading the Big Book and praying. Somehow I got through. One really bad night, when I couldn't stand watching him drink any longer, I went over to the hotel gift shop. They had a plaque on the wall I'd never seen before. It was the Serenity Prayer. And things like that just kept happening. . . .

If you are married or in a relationship when you begin to recover, you don't have the luxury of taking time. When you're half of another couple, you're there with the other person.

Among the qualities that lead to good relationships are flexibility, getting to know yourself, and being articulate. Which brings us to

Denial

For most of our lives, it's been to our advantage to deny reality. If we didn't, then how could we drink?

Think of denial like layers of an onion — from surface to the deep inner core.

Surface denial is like the man I recently read about in the paper. He was driving on the freeway when he saw a rocking chair in the middle of the road. It was just sitting there by itself, rocking gently. (It had fallen off a truck.)

---

*The Big Book is *Alcoholics Anonymous,* published by A.A. World Services, Inc., New York, N.Y.

I'm seeing things! he thought. And that's exactly what he told the police, after he'd driven right into it and caused a big jam on the freeway.

There's a psychological phenomenon in human beings. We deny what *doesn't fit in with our reality.*

When I was nine years old, I managed to convince myself that the neighbors who felt sorry for me really admired me for taking care of my family. The child of alcoholics grows up trying to fit in these "rocking chairs on the freeway." So often we live with chaos. We do the best we can. But this distortion of reality also distorts who we are and how we relate to others.

❋ ❋ ❋

I grew up telling lies. But to me it wasn't lying. It was survival. I said what I needed to say to avoid being beaten.

— Lois, thirty-eight

❋ ❋ ❋

Alcoholic parents often demand lies from their children. This was certainly true of my father. In our house, we were so intimidated by him that whatever he said was reality — even if it was totally illogical.

When we, as young adults, begin to date and enter relationships, our system of denial comes right along with us. Any alcoholic — and an alcoholic woman in particular — has a lot of trouble compromising and negotiating. Often, we're terrified of conflict!

Our fear of abandonment can be so strong that we view conflict as the beginning of the end. If there's going to be conflict, we think it means *I'm going to have to leave, or you're going to have to leave.*

We don't learn that *conflicts can be resolved without endings.* So much of our experience has been based on seeing conflict escalate until something terrible happens. We're haunted by too many ghost feelings.

Beyond denial, alcoholics and addicts frequently don't have boundaries.

Our parents' behavior may have fluctuated between extremes — like Carmen's mother who raged at and beat her children, and then, when they were sobbing, gave them cookies. Without mooring, we begin to drift. Needing excessive amounts of love and reassurance, we lose the ability to grasp simple manners as well as the nuances of boundaries.

We crave attention, so we have to get close to others — and at the same time, we have to keep our defenses up. We're so anxious to please! Like leeches, we attach; only the fiercest rejection will remove us.

Pia, a twenty-seven-year-old fabric designer, was born in Colombia and came to San Francisco with her parents when she was five. She remembers:

> We used to begin to get nervous when a certain cartoon show came on TV. That was when my dad was due home. My two brothers and I would begin to listen for the car, and then all three of us would watch from the window to see if our father would give away any signs of his mood.
> He was a construction worker and often stopped for drinks on the way home. His moods dictated what happened for the rest of the night. He was never physically abusive to us or our mom, but we had to tiptoe and "walk on eggs" because we all knew that something really bad was hanging over our heads.

The first time in her sobriety that Pia got into a relationship with a man, she began to feel edgy and watchful.

> In therapy, I began to see that I'd put another male authority figure in my life. And now I was watching his moods. So if Dan was tired or irritable, I became really

quiet and submissive. He thought this was weird! Eventually it made him angry with me!

I really don't know what I was waiting for. But it was something terrible.

Of all the characteristics and habit patterns we bring into relationships in sobriety, perhaps the most difficult are unresolved feeling states. That may sound like a fancy term, but it simply means that

- we drank and used to change our feelings.
- the events that *produced* those feelings were unfinished, unresolved.

For example, losses. Most of us have experienced significant losses. People we loved died, or left us, or moved away. All too frequently, we altered our natural feelings of loss, pain, and anger by drinking and using. Or perhaps we did it by eating, or having sex, or throwing ourselves into work.

By distorting our natural feeling states — by not allowing our mind to let our body "work through" them — we are left with unresolved conflict.

Failing, in particular, to deal with abuse, abandonment, incest, and emotional distress produces shame. And guilt.

In sobriety, as we begin to *experience* these unresolved feeling states, we may feel that those around us are responsible. In particular, we may feel that our partner in a relationship is the cause of emotional turmoil. That probably isn't true. It's far more likely that we have projected the characters (and feelings) from the past into our present, along with all the anxiety and turmoil that accompanied the original experiences!

In early recovery, we need to take a long, hard, realistic look at all of our past relationships. What were their strong points? What were their weak ones? Can we recognize a pattern in them?

While we are doing this, we need to back off, both from forming new relationships or from making any major changes in a relationship that already exists, until our recovery is stabilized.

The euphoria of a new relationship — the excitement of starting fresh — may vanquish our "ghosts" for a while. But just as the picture of an old TV can't be adjusted for very long, so our ghost feelings return in sobriety to haunt us or to destroy a new relationship.

By now, I'm sure you've noticed an echo running through all these chapters:

In Recovery — Take Things Slowly

We can get so lost while we're drinking. The women we really are vanish. And the elements of this disease in which we lose our real selves, are the same ones that destroy our relationships:

- dishonesty
- deception
- fear of intimacy
- fear of rejection
- low self-esteem
- previous abuse — sexual, physical, and emotional
- consistent compromises (people-pleasing behaviors to the extent that we make so many compromises, we've no idea what we really want)

The list could go on and on. Perhaps this is the place for you to make your own list — to begin to look at the character defects that recovery reveals, to write down some of the problems that were your contributions to turmoil in past relationships.

Part of recovery is to discover the answers to such questions as, "Who am I?" "What do I want from a relationship?" "What kind of partner do I want?" "What can *I* bring to a relationship?"

Lists help. The "husband list" I made as a graduate student — the one that led to The Chapel of The Bridal Wreath in Reno — was actually a good thing to do. But a list only works if you are honest and sober.

Another list that may help you is a list of how you want to *feel* in a relationship.

My own sponsor, Patt, tells me often, "It's all about feelings. What matters is knowing how you want to feel and being with someone who allows you to feel that way. It's not about anything else."

Do you want to feel frightened, lonely, embarrassed, and "less than. . . "? Don't be too quick to say, "Of course not!" These feelings may be familiar to you and have become comfortable.

In sobriety, it takes time to know how you *do* feel, let alone how you want to feel. Give yourself plenty of time.

Also, in early sobriety, it's often difficult to list anything good about ourselves! If you are making a list of what you have to bring to a relationship, you may think something like, *Sure, I'm an honest person. But I've done a lot of lying lately.* Or, *Yes, I'm witty and fun. But I don't feel that way now.* It's very important to list the positives in our inventory as well as the areas that can be improved.

We are now getting into an exciting area of recovery. Because building a list of what we have to give to a relationship is very much like building a dowry, a hope chest. Not a hope chest with linen, crystal, and silver — but with our human values and attributes. A hope chest that includes very valuable feelings. Our feelings.

The exciting part of sobriety is that it's a transformation process. We grow. It's a gradual process — as gradual as if we are a butterfly emerging from a chrysalis — but the growth is predictable.

And that's the beauty of sobriety.

Those of us who have been in recovery for a while know that the progress of recovery is just as predictable as the progress of the disease.

CHAPTER SEVEN

Give! Give! Give!
Our Emotional Conditioning

Sugar and spice, and everything nice. That's what little girls are made of.

— Old Nursery Rhyme

Building a sense of self-esteem and confidence in your daughter is a long-term responsibility of parenting. Begin when she is very young and make a point of continuing throughout her life. Your support will help her develop self-confidence, the first step toward becoming a person who cares enough about herself to avoid drug problems.

— KAREN BANKSTON and DOUGLAS WHITE
From *After Sugar and Spice*
(a manual for parents
about daughters, drugs,
and prevention)

* * *

In a small seaside town in California, a late-afternoon mist drifts over the fields behind the Fairmont Elementary School. The year is 1965, and eight-year-old Terry has stayed after class to feed the third grade's pets. (Two turtles, two white rats, and a hamster named Elvis.)

As she leaves the classroom, she sees Tommy Boynton standing at the end of the corridor.

Tommy!

The kids call him "Tommy the Terrible." Last Friday, she'd seen him drop a kitten out of a third-floor window. When she'd rushed over to rescue it — it was struggling to crawl away with both its back legs broken — Tommy had knocked her down, seized the kitten and run back to drop it from the window again.

She hates him.

He's blocking her way.

It's very quiet in the corridor. Where is everyone? The teachers never go home this early. The janitor, Mr. Jeffreys, is nearly always around. Shreds of mist are filtering through the open door behind Tommy, filling the air with a damp seaweed smell. She can hear her own breathing.

"Hi, Tommy," Terry says cautiously.

"Terry, Terry, fell off the ferry," Tommy chants. His hand shoots out and yanks up the hem of her dress. "You've got lace panties on."

"Stop that!" Terry shouts. To her horror, she sees that Tommy is now scrawling TERRY ANDREWS WEARS LACE PANTIES on the wall by the janitor's cupboard.

Red ink!

Everyone will see.

Anger flares inside Terry. She snatches the magic marker pen out of Tommy's hand. He grabs for it, yelling, "Baby! Baby! You cry in class."

Terry punches him in the face. It feels so good! A startled look flickers across Tommy's face. She punches him again, and suddenly he's on his back and she's sitting on top of him, sitting astride his chest, punching and punching. That's for the kitten, Tommy! Punch! Punch! He's kicking her, but she's too angry to feel it. Bright blood streams from his nose. Her head rocks as his fist smashes against her ear.

"Terry!"

The horrified voice of Mrs. Larch booms above her as Terry feels herself yanked upwards.

"*Tommy — go straight home, and have your mother clean you up,*" *Mrs. Larch is saying.* "*And you, young lady, come with me. I've never seen such disgraceful behavior in a little girl.*"

The teacher's lounge is overheated and reeks of stale coffee. Mrs. Larch's lips, thin and faintly etched with cyclamen lipstick, are clamped into a line of disapproval as she tugs and pulls at Terry's torn clothing. She will, she says grimly, have to call Terry's mother about Terry's disgraceful behavior.

Thoughts tumble around Terry's mind. Isn't Tommy's behavior disgraceful too? Why was he allowed to go home? Why wasn't Mrs. Larch calling his mother?

"*Tommy started it. He's a horrible boy, Mrs. Larch,*" *Terry says.* "*He's cruel. He tortured a kitten!*" *Mrs. Larch, still tugging and muttering, doesn't seem to hear her. Just as Terry's mother is always doing, she carries on talking as if Terry hadn't spoken at all.*

"*Little ladies,*" *she says,* "*do not stoop to fighting. What will your poor mother think when she sees you? She always sends you to school looking as if you'd just stepped out of a magazine.*"

Terry feels a lump rising in her throat. It's so unfair. Tears fill her eyes, spill over and roll down her cheeks — a final humiliation.

Mrs. Larch's voice softens. "*Well, now, it's not exactly the end of the world, dear. I'm sure you're never going to do anything like this again.*" *She pats Terry's shoulder.* "*A nice bath, a good night's sleep, and tomorrow you'll be sweet, pretty Terry again. . . .*"

❉   ❉   ❉

In all the years that Terry was growing up, no one taught her an acceptable way to express anger. She was never encouraged to make assertive statements, to verbalize angry feelings.

This type of emotional conditioning forces a child to distrust just how real his or her own feelings are, to replace a spontaneous response with one that society says is more acceptable. Terry, like so many of us, learned to keep her anger inside. To stuff it down. To be silent.

* * *

Silence was always my way of coping with my father's anger. I'd sit at the dinner table, silent, with tears in my eyes. I wasn't allowed to be angry. I never learned how to argue. How to say no.

— PAT B., twenty-seven

My mother would drink heavily for a week while the house fell apart around us. Then she'd rush around in a cleaning frenzy, screaming "Look what I have to do for you kids! You're not worth it. When I die, you'll never get such a nice mommy."

— MARY, forty-two

Living with my father was like walking on eggs. One day, he'd be kind; the next, raging. I remember once asking him if I could have my allowance a day early. "You want money?" he shouted. "I'll give you money!" And he pulled all the money out of his pockets and hurled it all over the yard.

— ANDREA, forty-two

* * *

You were fortunate as a child if what went on in your family provided you with the kind of personal conditioning that led to independence and self-esteem. Your family likes you. *You* like you!

Alcoholics and addicts often have the kinds of childhoods that — *one way or another* — condition us to have low self-esteem.

For me, emotional conditioning began with my father, and that's true for so many women.

It didn't take very long for my father to give me the message that life was unpredictable. He would hit his children with any implement within his reach if he became angry enough to lose control. His moods changed from sociable to violent with laser-like speed.

We were driving home from a family picnic once, when I was about twelve. We seemed right then to be just what I had always wanted — a perfectly normal family. My father was in a good mood. I was completely off guard.

Suddenly he began criticizing my best friend. Without really thinking, I said, "Oh, shut up about it."

He immediately became so violent that he let go of the wheel and lunged back over his seat to hit me. The car swerved wildly. My mother screamed and grabbed the wheel. As the car shuddered to a halt by the side of the road, my father dragged me out and began beating me over the head. I thought he was going to kill me!

My mother, although I didn't realize it, was dying by then. I felt so much anger toward her — for being weak, for being unable to protect me, for causing me so much work — instead of doing the things that other children's mothers did. But that anger was unacceptable. How could I hate my own mother? And for being sick? I began to believe that my feelings were unacceptable. I mistrusted my natural emotional reactions, and I began to second-guess myself — to react to my reactions.

Poor emotional conditioning leads to very low self-esteem. You can't trust yourself. You can't trust your own judgment. Your perceptions, due to this constant reacting to your reactions, seem to you to be different from other people's, so you feel worthless. Others seem to have so much more than you do in terms of judgment, common sense, the ability to get what they want.

You feel damaged in some way.

I continued to feel this way even later, when I was a successful and highly educated adult. I responded to everything emotionally — denying my intellect, my learning, my experience. I could easily have grown up to be a doormat, except that striving to please my father, I became fiercely competitive in athletics. In everything. I won swim meets. Essay contests. Beauty contests. But he never showed up to see me win anything. When, at sixteen, and two years ahead at school, I asked him for money for college, he said, "Women don't need to go to college. It's not worth the money." Instead, he offered me the price of a six-week secretarial course.

But I was determined to get an education, so I worked full-time hours though I was still in high school — and I saved every penny.

My Kentucky relatives, two alcoholic aunts and an assortment of nonfunctional uncles and cousins, had known for years about the abuse my brothers and I endured. Nobody intervened.

An aunt told me, "You can live with me while you're in college, if you can support yourself."

Looking back, it's difficult to describe how hard it was. I worked constantly. As a baby-sitter. Cleaning. Writing term papers. In two years, I saved enough money to pledge a sorority and move into a house. I longed to belong, to be like the other girls. To fit in.

They were girls reared for southern family life. And by my senior year, I was, like the other girls, determined to have a husband before graduation.

I first saw my husband-to-be walking up the gangplank at a riverboat party. He was twenty years old, a year older than me, and so handsome, with his crisply pressed army uniform and his dark curly hair, that all my friends wanted him. (Naturally, the competition inspired me.)

When we eloped across the state line, I sincerely believed I was going to create a real family. Above all, I wanted that picture-perfect family, including babies.

And I wanted someone to love, someone safe to love. So our married life began.

We were both working students. (I had a teaching job that paid the fantastic salary of three thousand dollars a year.) With the GI bill to buy a house, we seemed set. The forerunners of yuppies! It didn't occur to me that David was bringing his emotional conditioning, his expectations, into the marriage. Our goals were completely different. David was easygoing. It infuriated me when I discovered that he thought nothing of cutting classes to hang out with his buddies in the local bars.

Getting ahead in life had so little importance to him that — at a time when I was juggling college, two babies, and my part-time job — he turned down a promotion because he didn't want "the responsibility."

My emotional conditioning said, Win. Win. Win.

I felt that I *had* to "look good." That if my home wasn't perfect . . . if, for instance, I took the baby to church with a run in my stocking, people would see not only the run in my stocking but the run in my soul.

In both my marriages, I tried to be perfect at everything. The perfect homemaker. The perfect career woman. The perfect party-giver. But it was only by winning, by building constant successes that I felt I was worth loving and maybe worth keeping around.

And the anger, all my stuffed-down anger, waited.

If we've had poor or abusive emotional conditioning, and we also have a biological vulnerability to alcoholism, the two combine and cause us to feel things with alcohol and other drugs that we cannot feel without them. With alcohol, we discover we can feel all the things that we haven't learned to feel on our own.

When I was growing up, I knew, in the midst of all my emotional confusion, that winning an award was *good*. Straight A's were *good*. Winning any type of prize was *good*. These materialistic achievements were what my entire self-esteem was based on. The awards validated my being.

Many alcoholic women do the same thing, and many of us translate it into the way our physical outsides look.

And that's really the heart of "looking good."

Many of us know our insides are not to be trusted! Make-up, new clothes, well-behaved children, or spotlessly clean houses protect us. They make a statement to the world that somebody cared enough to buy nice things for us — or that we are important enough to be able to create these things for ourselves.

* * *

*I was so concerned about pleasing my father that, way
into my working life, when I was in my twenties, I had my
bosses writing to him to let him know that I was doing
wonderfully. He had to know.*

— MARJORIE, sixty-four

*I always wanted to be a doctor. My father said, "No,
be a nurse. It will fit you for marriage better."*

— MARY, forty-two

* * *

If, as part of your familial conditioning, you were taught to
make compromises, not waves, the reality is that at some
point, your disease brings you to alcohol and other drugs to
make those compromises bearable, to enable you to cope.

Sometimes it's a relationship that eases us over the border-
line into alcoholism — particularly if the relationship intro-
duces us to a lifestyle that centers around drinking.

* * *

We had one of those Days of Wine and Roses *marriages. It was fun, at first. My husband was an attorney,
and he didn't want me to work. Every day, at 5:00 P.M.,
I'd mix two martinis for us to drink when he got home. Of
course, if he was late, I'd drink them both myself and mix
some more. Attorneys work very long hours.*

— PAM, early forties

* * *

Many of us move from home into relationships without
missing a beat. If we come from dysfunctional homes, we
usually go into that first serious relationship *without having
questioned the value system we grew up in.*

Marina, who is now forty-three, had parents who treated her like a plaything. Her mother used to dress her up like a beautiful doll and hand her over to her father. He used to take her to bars. (He'd sit her on the bar and say things like, "Look, what a pretty girl!")

When Marina grew older, she looked for men who would take care of her. One night, when she was fifteen, she drank too much and passed out. Her boyfriend, in an act far more paternal than the usual teenage lover, carried her up to bed and tucked her in. A few years later, when he was a medical student, she married him.

She moved from her father to her husband, and found exactly the same thing. Her husband treated her like a child. She remembers:

> *The very first job I got was when I'd been married for sixteen years. I had no self-esteem. No confidence in my ability to earn money. At that time, I'd been sober for seven years, and I got a little job at a May Company that had just opened up.*
>
> *When I came home and told my husband I'd been hired he said, "They hired you? Well, did you tell them who your husband is?"*

* * *

Drinking helps us *not* to feel things, too — painful things, such as all that fear we've been stuffing down. Fear of not being good enough. Fear of losing in the intense competition for love.

Then, in recovery, as we begin to have insight into how our emotions were conditioned, we can come to a momentous, wonderfully exciting awareness. . . .

* * *

"*Where have you been all this time?*" *Jeff is saying to Terry as they edge down the buffet table at his sister's wedding.* "*You were gone nearly an hour!*"

"*I met your aunt. The children's book editor. She's fantastic....*"

"*You were talking to her for an* hour?"

"*Mmmhm.*" *Terry is feeling so much better about herself that it spills over into her feelings for Jeff. She gives his left ear a quick kiss. The buffet appears to be a mixture of Mexican dishes and California cuisine.* "*Those crab-in-pastry things look good, Jeff.*"

"You look good."

A few yards away from them, a troupe of Mexican mariachis, four men dressed in the black, silver-trimmed "suit of the horseman," have begun to play music. Strains of "Amor del Alma" mingle with the conversation of guests and the savory smells from the buffet.

I feel happy, *Terry thinks.*

I feel happy!

I'm going to be like Lindsay. That's what I want. That inner calmness she has. Her self-assurance. Her warmth. She has so much dignity....

Mr. Burton, Jeff's father, is approaching, smiling, holding out two wine glasses filled with a pale golden liquid.

"*It's Chateau d'Yquem,*" *he explains proudly.* "*Wine of gold. Your mother says the cost will ruin us — but how often does Karin get married?*"

"*Oh, no thank you, Mr. Burton,*" *Terry says. Seeing that he looks disappointed — his wonderful treat refused — she smiles, and adds,* "*I would if I could, but I'm a recovering alcoholic.*"

Jeff's hand clamps around her upper arm with such fierceness that she winces.

"*Why did you say that?*" *he hisses as his father heads in the direction of other guests.* "*You promised me you weren't going to tell anyone.*"

"*But ... but ...*" *How can she explain? How can she get him to understand that Lindsay has made her feel that a recovering woman can embody qualities of courage and dignity. She's so tired of lies!* "*When I was talking to your aunt ...*"

118

"Never mind my aunt! What's my father going to think? You embarrassed the hell out of me just now!" His voice goes on and on. Terry retreats into silent anger.

On the forty-minute drive home, neither of them speak. It's dark by the time they pull into her driveway. Light from the children's bedroom is spilling out across her neglected lawn. Is her mother up there with Cody? Although it's only a few minutes past nine, she'll probably get a lecture about being out "all hours of the night."

Beside her Jeff sighs. "Well, it's not the end of the world, I guess. My father probably won't say anything. But promise me you won't do this again?"

Something stirs at the back of Terry's mind. A memory? An echo? What is it? Suddenly, she has it! Mrs. Larch! She can almost feel the teacher's thin fingers tugging and pulling at her clothes as she mutters, "Well, now, it's not exactly the end of the world, dear. I'm sure you're never going to do anything like this again. A nice bath, a good night's sleep, and tomorrow you'll be sweet, pretty Terry again. . . ."

At that moment, sitting in Jeff's car, Terry reached a momentous awareness. She realized that all her life, someone — her mother, her teachers, her husband — had been conditioning her emotions, controlling them, forcing her to stuff her real feelings down.

And now Jeff was trying to do it too!

It was at that moment Terry made a choice: the choice that she was no longer going to stuff down her true feelings. No one was going to kill her spirit.

CHAPTER EIGHT

Hard Choices: Our Work and Our Dual Roles

"You mean there's an extra four hundred dollars an acre in growing costs alone?" Terry is asking over the phone. The humming clatter of the huge newspaper office surrounds her like familiar background music. The deep voice of the apple farmer she is interviewing — a surprising cheerful voice for a man facing bankruptcy — booms into her ear.

"What are your plans now?" she asks this man caught in the crunch since the furor over using Alar on apples hit more than a year ago. She scribbles furiously as the deep voice rumbles on about pruning strategies, about overhead sprinklers. She's recording the call, but she knows it's an in-office joke that she never quite trusts machinery.

Pinned to the edge of the shelf above her computer, a card from Jeff shows a smiling, dancing hippopotamus, mouthing the words "I'm Sorry." The card is a souvenir from the argument they had after his sister's wedding. The argument had been followed by a three-day split-up, then by a passionate reunion.

Last night, as they were curled up in bed together, Jeff had murmured against her hair that of course her feelings were important. So why does she have the uncomfortable feeling that he's just humoring her?

Work! Work! She must keep her mind on her work!

"Thank you, Mr. Hansen . . . thank you very much for your time," she tells the grower of apples, far away on his New England

121

farm. "I'll be sure to send you a tearsheet of the article. And, Mr. Hansen . . . er . . . best of luck!"

Terry puts down the phone and stares down at her notes without really seeing them. The sexual chemistry between Jeff and her is fantastic. Would she be an idiot to break things off? He has no idea of what her recovery program involves. But, then, how could he? He's never been to a recovery group in his life. Perhaps she's being unfair to him by expecting him to understand her program only through her interpretation of it?

Relationships are so complicated!

Thank God, her favorite women's meeting is at noon today. She can hardly wait to get there! She really feels the need to share her feelings. To share them with other women who understand.

As she types, "These days, when Rafe Hansen looks at his apple orchard . . ." into her computer, she smells the peppermint-lemon after-shave of her boss, Sheldon Davis. From the corner of her left eye, Sheldon's shirt is a dazzling blue-and-white-stripped blur. His hand presses her shoulder firmly as he snaps, "Terry. My office. Now."

Sheldon is a man who always sounds angry, even when he isn't. As she follows him into his office, Terry thinks he looks fiercely handsome, lean from daily jogging, the opposite of the baggy-pants, cigar-smoking stereotype of a big city editor.

"Ed Hadley just called me," he says. "Remember him?"

How could she forget!

Terry nods, trying to look calm. "Yes, the man who makes fiberglass fake food for restaurant displays. He was one of my Unusual Entrepreneur series two years ago."

She remembers interviewing Ed, drinking their way through lunch together on a rainy afternoon. By 3:00 P.M., they had been the only customers left in the restaurant. She must have been matching him, drink for drink. She has a vague memory of his hand sliding over her knee, creeping up her thigh, but no memory at all of how the afternoon had ended.

Had she gone back with him to his hotel? She has no idea, but it seems horribly likely that, yes, she probably did.

Sheldon is passing her a manila folder, explaining briskly that Ed Hadley appears to be doing very well these days. Very well indeed. His latest invention, some kind of fiberglass hybrid, is possibly about to revolutionize the car industry. Certainly, he rates an article.

"He asked specifically for you, Terry."

Of course he had! He must have been very comfortable being interviewed by a journalist who wanted to drink, who needed to drink, as much as he did.

"He's leaving for Tokyo in four hours," *Sheldon is saying.* "Your interview's at the Catamaran, at noon."

"I have, um, plans at lunchtime, Sheldon."

"Plans?"

"I've a meeting then. My woman's meeting."

She watches as, almost in slow motion, Sheldon's neatly brushed black eyebrows rise above his dark blue eyes. "AA?" *he asks.* "We're talking about an AA meeting? Don't those things go on all the time?"

"Well, yes, but . . ."

Sheldon is standing now, looming behind his desk, a certain indication that this business is concluded.

"For crying out loud, Terry, this is your job. Get your priorities straight."

Her priorities? Back at her desk, Terry huddles over her coffee mug and wonders what exactly those priorities are. Her friends in the program always tell her to put her sobriety first.

The voices of her co-workers keep interrupting her thoughts. "Hey, Ter . . . what happened to the photos of Trump Plaza?"

"Terry, angel child, can you cover my phone for the next ten minutes?"

"Terry, by any chance do you have a phone number for what's-his-name . . . that eccentric guy who walks around town with a robot?"

Her sobriety must come first! It was the difference between choosing life and death. What did other working people do?

Suddenly she remembers Lindsay. She's been a recovering alcoholic in the working world for ten years, *Terry thinks. But*

Lindsay was a busy editor. Surely it would be an imposition if she called her at her publishing house?

"No, You're not bothering me at all," Lindsay says when Terry reaches her. "I'm glad you called."

Just hearing Lindsay's voice lifts Terry's spirits. She explains the problem of Ed Hadley. The problem of her "history" with Ed. Her need to get to her women's meeting.

"Terry, what working people do is usually what they have to do," Lindsay says. "It's not enough to be sober. We have to be a part of the real world."

Terry feels a flash of annoyance.

"The 'real world,' Lindsay, doesn't seem to make any allowances for the fact that I'm an alcoholic! I mean, if I was recovering from cancer, my editor wouldn't say, 'You don't need to go to your chemotherapy session today.' He would probably offer to drive me over to the hospital!"

"What do you think you should do?" Lindsay asks calmly.

"What do I think?" Terry pauses. Now as she thinks about it, the answer seems obvious. "I guess I should do the interview. I can go to a meeting tonight."

As she thanks Lindsay and hangs up the phone, Terry feels strangely calm. It's a wonderful feeling. Suddenly she feels as though she could cope with anything. What on earth, she wonders, smiling, has happened to her? She feels like she's practically floating, about to drift up over her desk like a birthday balloon! Is this what they call a spiritual experience? Is this how it works?

✳ ✳ ✳

At work now, I have these little rushes of personal power.

> — PAT, twenty-seven,
> A civil engineer, sober
> for twenty-two months

✳ ✳ ✳

When we begin to realize that we can cope, that we have developed strengths in our program that will see us through anything, it's exciting!

Terry has made huge strides in the four months since she sat in her too-tight shorts, whining in her mother's kitchen. Her life is turning into an adventure, not a burden.

In early sobriety, however, when we first return to the real world of work, that world can be a very slippery place for us.

*   *   *

I hear people who come into the program say, "I'm going to take a year off work while I'm getting myself straightened out." How can they afford it? I had five children and my husband had left. I had to keep on working.

— JAN, late forties

*   *   *

I also had to return to work early, after just a few meetings. My attitude when I first went back to work, was that because I was a recovering alcoholic, people were going to treat me with great kindness. They were going to let me do anything I wanted. If I wanted to wander off and read the Big Book in the middle of the morning, well, everyone else would sort of back away and put a protective shell around me.

It wasn't that way at all.

Nothing had changed. The pressures were just the same. The pace was the same. The phones were still ringing. Nothing had stopped because I got sober. In fact, no one had even noticed.

*   *   *

The first job I had after I got sober was in public relations. I got fired three months later. I'd never been fired before. It brought out such rage! I thought, How could they do this to me? I'm a recovering alcoholic with three months sobriety, and I'm wonderful. *I wanted to drive my car straight into their wall.*

— JAN, late forties

* * *

In early recovery, while I was still in a state of detoxification, I found it very difficult to work. I used to try and hide the fact that my hands were shaking. I would read the same paragraph over and over without comprehending its meaning. It was almost impossible to concentrate.

I felt, in fact, like a convalescent who ought to be laying on a lounge chair, wrapped in a blanket. (Now I feel that I was probably much better off working than staying at home.)

After the first stage of our recovery has passed and, as Terry is doing now, we begin to realize that we can cope, work still holds special challenges for us. Because, somewhere along the line, most of us also realize that much of our drinking behavior was actually learned at work. We have modeled our drinking after the patterns of others — frequently men in positions of authority.

Jan, who rarely drank more than the odd glass of wine until she was thirty, remembers:

I learned to drink in my first job. I was a press aide on the governor's staff. Everyone around me was drinking scotch, and I learned to like it. I was a social drinker at first. Then, as my marriage started to unravel, I began drinking heavily. I saw myself as I'd always been — slim, attractive, and successful. I didn't realize I was slowly turning into a bloated drunk.

In 1987, I did a study of how women's jobs influence them to drink. It was a survey of 100 women in two large corporations. Nearly half of them reported using alcohol to relax after work, and more than half sometimes drank at lunch. Interestingly, the same women who wouldn't think of drinking on a coffee break didn't consider drinking at lunch and returning to work in the same light. There was no real understanding that if you drink alcohol at lunch, you are returning to work with your judgment impaired.

But is it work that causes drinking?

I remember how many times I would be the one to organize going out to lunch during the workday. Because addiction and alcohol problems are conditions not only of social acceptability, but of denial, I was always trying to find others who behaved as I behaved. It helped me to justify my own behavior.

"Mmm, I feel like Mexican food today," I'd murmur casually to a co-worker. "Maybe a green chile burrito."

The reply was usually along the lines of, "Yeah — that sounds good. Where do you want to go, Ann? Tortilla Alley?"

"No, let's go to The Ristra," I'd say. "I think the service is so much better." (This dialogue really said, "Tortilla Alley doesn't serve drinks. The Ristra does.")

Being with a client makes it easy to rationalize drinking. How often have you heard one or more of the following?

- "Sales people *have* to drink with clients."
- "If you had my deadlines, you would drink too."
- "If you had to work with these people, you would need a booster too."
- "A few drinks at lunch calms me down, so I can be more focused after a tense morning."
- "I would never get to sleep without my 'nightcap' — the many details of work just keep spinning and spinning around in my head."

And on, and on. . . .

❊ ❊ ❊

She was like any other housewife, fixing dinner by the light of a martini.

— MONICA DICKENS, author

* * *

Working sometimes provides us with more "reasons" to drink than if we are working at home. If you are drinking with a client at lunchtime, you are going to have an entirely different image of yourself than if you are drinking in your kitchen, with your baby sitting next to you in a high chair.

* * *

My grandmother didn't start drinking until she was in her late seventies. She went down fast, but, at that stage, we weren't sure if it was the alcohol or her age. When she was younger, she never had the opportunity to drink. She lived on a farm, and on her visits to town she would have thought it scandalous to be seen going into a bar!

— DANIELLE, thirty-one

* * *

In previous generations, women who were susceptible to this disease were often kept out of the bars by social taboos. Now, it's often the opposite. Our work often gives us many opportunities to drink, without providing us with

Education About the Dangers

Normal drinkers, invited to go along with co-workers for the 5:00 P.M. happy hour, will soon recognize how silly others get after an hour or so of drinking. After a while, they'll start thinking, *Why do I want to waste time hanging around listening to this?* They'll pull away. Or perhaps they'll limit it to just Fridays. Normal drinkers have lots of other things they want to do besides drinking.

But the alcoholic woman, who feels like a different person when she drinks, is going to love the Happy Hour! It feeds perfectly into her denial system. It's okay to be doing this. "Everybody" at work is doing it. And no matter what happens during the day, no matter how hectic or frustrating or tense things get at work, she now has that wonderful moment to look forward to — when she can relax with a drink.

And It Accelerates the Progress of Her Alcoholism

Eventually, as her problems accelerate too, alcohol begins to seem like her only friend.

I always believed that I had to drink in order to survive whatever happened to be going on in my life. Many alcoholic women have told me that they felt this way. We drank to solve problems when, in fact, drinking was our problem.

* * *

My boss was going to ACA meetings. He recognized that I needed help, and he told me why I needed it.
— PAT, twenty-seven

* * *

There are bosses who would rather walk a mile barefoot over broken glass than confront an alcoholic employee, especially a woman. Many bosses not only don't recognize that an alcoholic woman needs help — or don't *want* to recognize that she needs help — but they may enable her to drink for their own reasons.

They may be alcoholic too.

Or they may feel lucky to have an employee so overqualified for the job that she takes on extra tasks.

* * *

At my six-month review, my boss said, "You have all the capability in the world! You're the only one who doesn't know that." My low self-esteem wouldn't allow me to know it. I used to burn the candle at both ends. I worked seven days a week. Then at night, I had false confidence — safe in the dim bars in my cowboy boots.
— PAT, twenty-seven

* * *

Driven by guilt — "My God, what did I *do* at that office party?" — or by panic — "I'm going to get fired!" — we often come in early and stay late.

In the later stages of my own drinking, when I was selling art, I used to wake up regularly at 3:00 A.M. as my body began to detoxify. Unable to sleep, I'd get up, get dressed, and be sitting at my desk by 4:00 A.M.

So, with all of our guilt, our fears, our low opinion of ourselves, we're often an easy target for a boss to manipulate.

It's not only male bosses who sometimes do this, who take advantage of an overqualified alcoholic woman with low self-esteem. I've done it myself. I didn't realize I *was* doing it. It goes back to the story of Mary Kay. . . .

I couldn't believe my luck when Mary Kay became my secretary. In a very short time, she also became my friend. She was so intelligent! Such a marvelously hard worker! She was also an alcoholic, but I wasn't about to face up to that. I mean, Mary Kay drank less than I did, so what did that make me? . . .

The two of us always went to bars for lunch. But to make things look "good," we took piles of work with us. We had papers all over the table. I was secure in my pretense that if anyone we knew walked by — as we were knocking back our third or fourth beer — they would think, *Oh, there's Ann and Mary Kay hard at work, as usual.*

One day Mary Kay — friend, secretary, drinking partner — didn't show up for work. I never saw her again. Months later I heard that she had gone back to her abusive, alcoholic husband. The two of them were often seen in the local bars.

❊ ❊ ❊

> *Sometimes I drank sitting on the cellar steps, in the dark. But my favorite place to drink was inside my closet. I kept my bottles in a Nordstrom's carrier bag, and I'd go and sit in there, among the hanging clothes, with only this little slit of light coming through the door. And no one could see me.*
>
> — JOYCE, sixty

❊ ❊ ❊

Mary Kay and I, out in the bars that served lunches, were doing the same thing that Joyce, in her dark closet, was. We were trying to cover up the fact that we were drinking.

So there I was, taking long lunch hours, exhibiting poor judgment, and justifying my insanity by coming to work at 4:00 A.M. I was what *I* would describe as a difficult employee. (A perfect candidate for an Employee Assistance Program referral, in fact.) But no one in authority ever confronted me. No one suggested that I was drinking too much.

Many alcoholics — both men and women — are valued by their bosses because they put in long hours. But our pattern of work is usually erratic. We work, as I did, on our own terms.

By the time I moved to Southern California and the job at The Wild Turkey restaurant, I was on my last legs, literally and figuratively. I was still trying to create that wonderful picture of a wonderful life, though, still struggling desperately to "look good."

I was dancing my eternal tap dance.

After the end of my waitress "career," I tried yet another job change, again seeking a solution to my problems through work. The first job I found was in a golf shop. (I justified being a Ph.D. who sold golf balls with jargon like "burn-out.") People had been telling me for years that I'd be terrific at sales. When this didn't work out, I repeated my pattern: I found another job, selling corporate art.

I seldom drank in public anymore. I couldn't trust myself. But by then I was at the point where if I didn't drink, I had to have *something*. So, like a lot of others who have found themselves caught in this trap, I took the "cocaine cure" to stop drinking.

Drugs had been a part of my juggling act since the beginning. I had begun taking Valium — my first prescription abuse — when I was eighteen. At that time, I thought I was having anxiety attacks, perhaps even a nervous breakdown. "Don't worry, these pills will handle your symptoms," the doctor assured me.

Two years later, when my first husband and I were newlyweds and driving cross-country, we were students, too broke to stop driving and stay in motels, so another doctor gave me Dexamyl to stay awake.

This began the prescription drug abuse, the "better living through chemistry," that affects so many women. Soon, it just became easier to get them from the streets. As a college professor, I bought drugs from my students.

By the time I was selling art, I was taking cocaine mixed with crystal every morning. It was the first thing I did when I got out of bed. It cut the shakes and got me going. Then I would overdose a little bit just before I got in the car. I'd have a hard time driving, of course, but I'd get out in the traffic and drive to the office like a horse with blinders on — a menace! By the time I got to work, I was straightened around, so I'd go into the public bathroom, hunch down on the stool with a small mirror on my lap, and snort a line through a dollar bill.

Gradually, my habit increased, until I was using as much as a gram a day. And they were long days — fourteen, sixteen, or eighteen hours. I needed amphetamines to keep my energy level up. Soon, I was taking so much cocaine and crystal that if I had even one drink with gallery clients, I was already ripped.

I had a whole repertoire of excuses. "I'm such a light drinker," I would say. "One drink just goes straight to my head!" Sometimes, I'd trot out the old line about being on prescription medication. Or I'd blame it on a diet: "No lunch, you know."

Much later, in recovery, I realized how I used my jobs, my work, to rationalize the use of many drugs. I was an addict.

It wasn't just the outside work that helped me to rationalize drinking and using. In early recovery, I, who had been cleaning things since I was old enough to get my fingers around a sponge, discovered that for me *housework* was a trigger for drug-dependent thoughts!

In my first year of recovery, it seemed overwhelming. So I did nothing. Behind dim windows, my dying plants drooped under a thick layer of dust. My floors grew sticky. The empty glasses under my king-sized bed — left over from my long-past last night of drinking — were growing mold under there! One day, through the fog I was in, a thought penetrated: My home was a mess!

I can remember standing on the landing of the stairs to the living room, gazing down at the disarray, and the thought came clearly: *Without cocaine, I'm never going to have enough energy to be able to have a clean house.*

And that made perfect sense to me!

A lot of these early fears are just part of the territory — part of the incredible confusion of early sobriety.

It Doesn't Last

In recovery, work can be a particularly confusing and slippery place for us. At work, we encounter many things over which we simply don't have a choice.

Most of us don't have a choice about going back to the same job — we are fortunate if we *have* a job to go back to —

and early recovery is not the time to make career changes. We are usually so debilitated in early recovery that we have enough to cope with, just hanging on to the job we've got. If we are married, coping with the same responsibilities and routines is enough of a challenge, without taking on new ones.

There are many slippery places to be wary about in your recovery. One I have found to be an important red flag is

---

The Temptation to Become Compulsive About Work

---

* * *

I still have a tendency to want to do it all. I have to consciously stop . . . to remind myself I can't. Some of it can wait for tomorrow. Or even next week.

— ANGIE, fifty-four
A bookkeeper
for an auto dealer

* * *

Work is such a temptation! Sometimes, it can give us immediate positive feedback. And early recovery is a time when we usually need a boost to our battered self-esteem.

Maybe, at this stage in your life, your home life is a mine field. Maybe your children are sulking because they can no longer manipulate you, as they did when you were drinking. Maybe your parents are being very cool to you because a few months before you hit bottom, you borrowed money from them to buy a car and blew it at Las Vegas.

At your work, however, by placing a priority on achievement, you can get some immediate gains. You can gain recognition for your abilities. Praise. A promotion. A raise.

Overwork is a temptation for any alcoholic — male or female — because of our obsessive tendencies.

The key is

Balance

Be aware of this slippery place by remembering, for us,

Extremes of Any Sort Are Dangerous

The second area that can be a red flag is

Where You Work

Mary, forty-two, a mental health counselor, has been in recovery for six years. She says:

> When I quit drinking and using cocaine, marijuana, crystal, Valium, and mushrooms on the weekend, I was interning at a large hospital where most of the staff were using something. That was our way of coping. We partied together too. We'd justify it by saying things like, "We deserve a little fun after the kind of stress we get working in this place!"
>
> I remember a lot of wild nights. One time I was drinking out in the hospital parking lot at 2:00 A.M. with this male nurse. For some reason, I was wearing a transparent nightdress. I said to him "What if somebody sees us?" And he said, "Well, if they can't take a joke. . . ." Then, the next morning, I was the "good" me again. It was like turning into a vampire every night! The conflict — the "good" me always picking up the pieces after the "bad" me — was very draining.

In sobriety, I stayed in the same job. At first, it was very difficult. People had got used to coming to me when they wanted drugs. In sobriety, I had to cut off every former friend I had.

Also, at the hospital, I'd been doing everyone's charting at the end of the day. I felt so guilty all the time — I mean, I was a mental health professional going out at night and picking up men in bars — so doing everyone's charting was a way of justifying my existence. In recovery, I said, "I can't do this anymore." At first, they got pretty upset, but I pointed out that it wasn't healthy for me — and they accepted that.

If a woman in new sobriety asked me for advice about her job, I'd tell her to take a look at where she was and try to see the pattern of using at work and how it tied in with her job.

Are you, perhaps, returning to work in a hospital? As a bartender? A cocktail waitress? At a restaurant, or a high-tech computer division where it seems as if almost everyone is taking the edge off stress with drugs and alcohol?

If any of your co-workers have been selling you drugs — or if you yourself were the dealer, it complicates the situation even further.

Many of us, like Jan, are fired from our jobs in early recovery. Some of us have no job to be fired from and are afraid that we may never have one again. Still others would like to put the marriage and kids on "hold" for the next few months. The future can look pretty bleak to us at this stage.

Joyce, who walked out of hospital detox on a rainy New Year's Eve after being in only seven days — "because I had no insurance," — remembers how low she felt.

I felt I was practically unemployable! I was in my fifties. And what do you put on a resumé when you've been fired from your last job for drinking?

*Two weeks later, I entered a recovery home run by the
Salvation Army. I met a woman there, Chris. She had
been in recovery for about four years and was doing very
well as the clothing manager for five stores. Chris hired
several of us to help her with inventory. For me, meeting
her was the first of a series of little miracles. After the
inventory was over, she said, "You did so well, Joyce.
Would you like to stay on?" Eventually, I became a
manager myself. It's wonderful in early recovery to work
for somebody who understands!*

Another red flag area for us is the one the title of this
chapter was drawn from:

The Choice Between Responsibilities at Home and at Work

---

*My attorney daughter told me she was so busy trying
to live up to the "Supermom" image she even lied to the
children that she had baked cookies for a Halloween school
party, when she really had bought them.*
— ELIZABETH KLUNGNESS

* * *

Maureen, who works for a radio station, has been in recovery for more than six years now. She was a "speed-freak" who
used alcohol to come down from a high. She says:

*My husband was using crack too. But he could take it
or leave it — he said.*
*I was so guilt-ridden about what was happening to me
that I'd come home every night — after a full day of sales
activities for the station — and make dinner for the kids.
Then I'd make a second gourmet, romantic meal for us!*

Luckily, his work kept him at late meetings many nights, so I'd frantically do all the housework, laundry, help the kids with their homework, and then my own stuff, to be calmly relaxing and loving by the time he got home.

"You're a marvel!" he'd murmur, as I poured more trendy wine for both of us. "I don't know how you do it."

He used to call me his "Enjoli" gal. Remember that ad?

When I quit drinking, it all fell apart. And it seemed they all turned against me. Of course, none of them — my husband or the kids — wanted to give up the good deal I had been giving them out of my own guilt!

Earlier, I mentioned the shame experienced by those of us who juggle too much to do. Shame is a great motivator. Women in the workplace have some very hard choices. Something's got to give. And the thing that usually has to give is our relationships.

In Recovery, You Need a Careful Plan Of Where You Are Going

Terry's decision to proceed with the interview with the hard-drinking entrepreneur illustrates that she was learning, at that point, to trust her program. It was a slippery place for her, but she put her recovery first, sought advice from someone (Lindsay) who had already experienced what she was going through, and took another step toward normalizing her life as a sober woman.

In sobriety, I returned to a profession of helping. I had to start at the bottom again, but I realized gradually that my jobs selling golf balls or art had been part of an escape, an escape from myself.

Starting again isn't easy. No matter where we are with our careers, our dual roles, and our relationships, the path to a full and balanced life will involve making hard choices to keep recovery in the forefront.

Our strength as recovering women is in unity with each other, our families, our children, our friends, and the men and women who love us. Our strength grows with support. Sometimes, that support may be given grudgingly, as we go through the challenges of turning from Superwomen back to human beings.

As this chapter concludes, continue with your own story. To help your growing awareness, write out a mini-inventory. Consider the following:

1. Your job. Is it salaried or not? How do you feel about it? Is it meeting your needs? Perhaps career counseling or more education may be a next step.
2. Why are you in this job? (Be realistic. Often money is necessary until you can make a plan.)
3. Has drinking been entwined with your work in any way?
4. List the co-workers you drank with, including those who enabled you by lying for you or supporting your version of reality.
5. Examine any "can'ts" that may change how you function or other people's expectations of you. For example, Terry cannot be a drinking companion while she conducts interviews. I found that, without the extra energy chemicals gave me, I could no longer work without a lunch break or work on weekends. What are some of the expectations other people — including spouses and children — may have of you that you can no longer meet?
6. Has saying no to anything, including overtime, been a problem since you returned to work in sobriety? Share at recovery meetings any stress, any conflict, you may be experiencing. Share the guilt you may be feeling.

Remember, the juggling act of the Superwoman may involve some breakage when she stops catching all the plates! But, for this time, put yourself and sobriety first!

CHAPTER NINE

Hitting Bottom: Illusion and Reality

I hit bottom when I no longer believed my own lies.
— My friend Ron M.

* * *

For the third time in a week, Terry sits on a hard folding chair in the gym of her local YMCA, listening to a recovery meeting. This one is a discussion meeting. The topic is "Hitting Bottom."

"I had reached the point where I didn't even have a car to live in," Henry, a sixty-seven-year-old retired plumber, is saying. "My wife had thrown me out. I hadn't worked for about a year. I was living under a bridge."

Terry stares at Henry, standing at the podium with his stooped shoulders, his grayish face seamed by forty years of hard drinking. It's hard to imagine that she has anything in common with this man.

"I was starving," Henry is saying about the night he realized he had hit bottom. "I found this ham sandwich — well, half a ham sandwich — that someone had tossed away maybe three days earlier. The meat was smelly, slimy with decay...."

Nothing like that ever happened to me, Terry thinks, as Henry launches into a description of how he ate the sandwich. I've always had a home, good food, a nice car.

Her mind begins to drift back. It drifts to a humid summer morning, to waking up on her living room sofa.

She was still wearing the clothes she had been wearing the day before. Her gold bracelet had pressed a deep red ring into the flesh of her left arm. As she hauled herself upright to peer at the clock, she felt nausea rise in her stomach. There seemed to be something horrible going on inside her head too — a sloshing sensation, as though her brain was floating in liquid and might roll out of her head with any sudden movement.

It was five minutes past nine. She was late for a 9:00 A.M. staff meeting. Again.

That morning had definitely been a bottom for her. She can remember everything about it. . . .

. . . The house was too quiet. Had Ben got Beth off to school and Cody to the sitter? He must have. Had he been so angry that he hadn't even tried to wake her? The last thing she can remember was having a few drinks after dinner. To unwind.

In the bathroom, moving gingerly, she swallowed a couple of aspirins with tap water and splashed cold water on her face. Her eyes looked reddened, sore. She tried getting a drop of Visine into each of them, but her hands shook so much that most of the eyewash dribbled down her cheeks. From its perch on the bathroom shelf, the digital clock glowed ominously.

Fifteen minutes past nine.

Under the headache, under the nausea, Terry felt a growing sense of panic. Staffers who missed meetings without a valid reason were in trouble. She'd been late several times in the last couple of months. She'd invented too many excuses. Told too many lies. How many times could one woman have flu, or car trouble, or a sick child?

Twenty past nine!

At least she was already dressed. She peered down at the cream linen skirt, the green silk blouse, and cream waistcoat that she'd put on more than twenty-four hours ago. They were badly creased, but still clean enough. They'd do. She found a pair of shoes, grabbed her canvas work satchel, shakily poured a mug of coffee from the luke-warm pot in the kitchen, and ran.

The newspaper's underground parking garage was full. It always was by this hour of the morning. She was forced to drive, muttering under her breath, up and down all five levels twice, before she found a space. As she was pulling into it, her coffee mug toppled over into her lap. She looked down in despair at the large brown stain spreading across the front of her skirt. Now she was stained as well as crumpled! Don't panic, kid, *she thought.* Cold water will fix it. You just have to get to a bathroom.

The corridor to her office was lined with black and white photographs from feature stories. She was scurrying past them, holding her satchel over the stain, when the managing editor Brad Martin loomed in front of her.

"Brad! What a morning!" she cried. If she could get in the first word, maybe she could placate the man before he said anything. "My water heater exploded. It was like the Johnstown flood!"

The managing editor had a strange expression on his face. Usually, he looked formidably confident. Today he just looked wary. Uneasy.

"Terry," he said, "could you come into my office? I've asked Jean from Personnel to join us."

They were going to fire her!

Panic overwhelmed her. Fearful thoughts rushed wildly through her mind. If she lost her salary, they'd never make the house payment. Ben had just treated himself to that top-of-the-line Corvette. Their monthly bills were huge.

And her mother! *How would she ever be able to tell her mother she was unemployed? No one on her mother's side of the family had ever been fired, from anything.*

I won't tell her, *Terry thought.* I'll fake it 'til I find a new job.

From the managing editor's tenth floor office, the city spread out in a dazzling panorama of skyscrapers and the glittering water of the harbor. She sank gratefully into one of his black leather armchairs. They'd be crazy to fire her. She was too good at what she did. She was an award winner. She positioned her satchel carefully over the front of her skirt. There was a run in one of her stockings, but she managed to cover that by crossing her legs.

Jean, the personnel officer, was smiling at her. Smiling? Did people smile at you before they fired you? The sunlight slanting through the windows hurt her eyes. There was a strange ringing in her ears. *That had been happening to her a lot lately. Brad Martin was saying something. She squinted at him, trying to look composed.*

"*Terry, you've been a very valuable employee. . .*"

I need a drink, *Terry thought.*

"*. . . but in recent months we've noticed a severe decline in your work.*"

There was a restaurant in the lobby that served beer and wine. Depending on the elevators, it took about five minutes to get down there. . . .

Jean was talking now. She was talking about drinking. She was talking about missed appointments and late deadlines, about inaccurate quotes, follow-up calls that hadn't been made, and research that had been skimmed over. A litany of journalistic transgressions. She was talking about an Employee Assistance Program.

Did they want to put her *in one of those things? Mike on the city desk was in an EAP program. He had to go to AA meetings.*

My mother, *she thought,* would die if she found out I was going to Alcoholics Anonymous!

"*You'll have to see a counselor,*" *Jean said gently.* "*I've made an appointment for you this afternoon.*"

"*I hardly think that's necessary,*" *Terry said. She started to rise from her chair. Her satchel slid sideways, thudding softly onto the pale gray carpet. Two pairs of eyes — Jean's blue and Brad's hazel — fastened on the stain on the front of her crumpled skirt.*

Terry had a sudden mental image of how she must look to them. They weren't seeing her as an award-winning professional. A superachiever. Not anymore. The secret was out. They were seeing her as a pathetic drunk with a hangover, who was losing her grip.

It's all over, *she thought.* I've gone too far.

The ringing in her ears made her feel as though she were under water. Through a swirl of sound she heard, very faintly, her own voice saying, "*Okay. I'll go and see the counselor.*"

* * *

In the YMCA gym, Henry is finishing his talk with a story about waking up in a dumpster just in time to see a trash collection truck bearing down on him. Somehow, he manages to make the experience sound hilarious. Laughter and applause warm the room. He catches Terry's eye and winks at her. She feels his genuine love for this room full of other fellow recovering human beings.

How could she ever have thought she had nothing in common with Henry. We have everything in common, she thinks. We have both escaped.

* * *

When the policeman took out his handcuffs, I knew something had changed. I didn't know it then, but I was hitting bottom. It was a real moment of clarity for me.
— Taken from a story told
by a young girl who had
been arrested for drunk
driving

* * *

Every recovering alcoholic remembers when they hit bottom. Vividly.

When you go to any Twelve Step group meeting where hitting bottom is the topic, you'll hear as many definitions of it as there are speakers. You'll hear low-bottom stories like Henry's, and high-bottom stories from people like Terry who got into recovery before, relatively speaking, they had suffered many material losses.

You'll hear stories from people who hit bottom when no one around them even suspected they *had* a drinking problem. And stories from people whose turning point came after they woke up in jail, or married to a stranger, or with the bed on fire.

For many of us, like the young girl who was arrested for drunk driving, hitting bottom involved an event, a crisis, something that jarred us into

Seeing Ourselves Clearly

Others, like my friend Ron, who said he hit bottom when *he* no longer believed his own lies, describe the experience as an emotional reaction. This happens when we can no longer rationalize our irrational behavior to ourselves.

For me, hitting bottom began this way. It began with a basket of flowers.

It was the morning after a three-day holiday weekend, and I couldn't sober up enough to get out of bed and get to work. At the time, I had no idea that I was about to begin three weeks of torturous isolation that would lead me to a suicide attempt. I just knew that, right then, I couldn't stop drinking.

The all-too-familiar panic set in.

I called the art gallery where I worked and said, "I've just had some terrible news. My father has died! I'm catching a plane out to New Mexico this afternoon, so I'll be gone for several days."

I felt quite justified in lying. By that point, lies were my survival skill. Whatever I had to do to survive — and drink — I did. I figured that I would be able to get myself straightened around, somehow, if I could just have one more day to drink and make a fresh start the next day.

Several hours later, the doorbell rang. I ignored it, feeling another stab of anxiety hit me. I couldn't let anyone see me in this condition! It rang again.

I crept downstairs and peered through the peephole in my front door, just in time to see a delivery van pulling away. There was an expensive-looking basket of flowers sitting on the top step. A mistake? Who would be sending me flowers? Tucked into the side of the basket, I found a card from a co-worker, a woman named Liz.

"My Dear Ann," Liz had written. "I can't begin to tell you how sorry I was to hear about your father. . . ."

She went on to say that she knew how terrible I must be feeling, that it had been only a few months since she had lost her own father.

Her words were loving. Touching. Empathetic.

Then the reality of my lie hit me. It overwhelmed me. In my own eyes, I was lowered to a new level of degradation. It's one thing to lie to and manipulate someone you've just met in a bar — the odds are that they're also trying to manipulate you — but here it seemed like such a *cruel* lie. Liz was a good friend, a decent person. She had always seemed fond of me, and now she was showing me how much she cared by sharing her feelings of sorrow about a father she had loved. A father she had *really* lost.

I don't think I realized it then, but in the twenty/twenty hindsight of sobriety I see those flowers, that note, as the last kick in the stomach. The point where you think, *Well, I'm down, and I'm not getting up.*

It was the event that began the process of hitting bottom.

Whatever form hitting bottom takes, it always hits you in the solar plexus. It always hits hard. And it seems to mark us irrevocably — as though we've been touched by an invisible branding iron. Because we never forget it.

Hitting Bottom Serves the Function Of Giving Us Something to Build On — One Day at a Time

If you who are reading these words are still drinking and using, still trapped in the lies, the pain, the fear, the coverups, the eternal mad tap dance

It's Not Necessary for You to Go Down Any Further

It's not necessary for you to keep on enduring humiliation until you lose everything. You don't need to wait until lightning strikes. Allow that scorching fear that is inside you to come through now.

Allow that Secret to Come out Now Allow that Moment of Admission to Be Now

The longer we drink, the higher the price we pay. For me, that price almost meant leaving my two daughters with the memory of a mother who shot herself.

* * *

If I hadn't got sober I would never have seen my grandchild.

— SUZANNE, fifty-one

* * *

My friend Patt's turning point involved her grandchild.

Patt didn't think of herself as a problem drinker. She had a job, a nice home, and a family. She also had a husband, another alcoholic, with whom she partied and went to bars a lot. Patt drank alone, too, sometimes, but she always managed to be sober when she needed to be. She simply didn't feel her drinking was affecting anybody else.

One morning, after one of those boozy nights with her husband, Patt woke up on a mascara-smeared pillow with a crushing hangover. Her teased hair (this was years ago) was so matted she couldn't get a comb through it, and it hurt too much to try.

She had the house to herself — her husband had managed to get to work — so she dragged on a robe and crept into the kitchen to make a pot of coffee. She was leaning against the counter, trying not to move her head more than an inch in any direction, when her daughter Sharon and her three-year-old granddaughter Misty walked in through the kitchen door.

"Hi, Mom!" Sharon said brightly. "How are you doing?"

Then Sharon saw exactly how Patt was doing. Patt watched as both disgust and sadness mingled in her daughter's expression. "Not so good, huh, Mom," Sharon said softly.

Patt felt shaken. She also felt that she needed a drink. A beer. But she didn't want Sharon to know just how badly she needed it, that first drink of the day.

"I'm fine, honey, fine," she said. "I know I look like something the cat dragged in, but I've had a touch of that flu that's been going around. It's just about gone now. Do you want some lunch? Some lemonade for Misty? I think I'll have a beer. . . ."

Sharon turned to her three-year-old, took her hand, and said, "Come on, Sweetie. Grandma doesn't need us anymore."

As they started to walk out, Patt saw her whole life going out of the door. In that moment of clarity, she knew Sharon was right! What Grandma needed was a beer. She needed a beer more than she needed her daughter and granddaughter.

That was the turning point for her.

Eight years later when Patt, who by that time was my sponsor, told me this story, I identified with it instantly. I've seen that "look" so often in my own children's eyes.

Over the years, I'd often stopped drinking — for an hour, a day, a week. Toward the end, I actually stopped for longer periods of time. I had to, in order to get my health and everything else back together.

One time I managed not to drink for almost two weeks. My daughter Tandice, who was seventeen then and living with me, was really excited about it.

It's amazing, the fortitude of children. The eternal hope! They believe you when you say you've stopped completely. They believe you, of course, because they want so desperately to believe that now, finally, everything is going to be okay. No more clock watching, no more distraught thinking, *She's so late. What will she be like when she comes in? Where is she? Maybe she's passed out on the Smith's lawn again? Maybe she's had an accident with the car?*

On this particular evening, I'd been sober for thirteen days. Tandice was cooking dinner, and I was sitting at the counter that runs between the dining room and the kitchen, chatting to her, still dressed in the high-style clothes I wore at the gallery.

My mind fixed on a drink.

The obsession began working in me.

I needed a drink. A drink. A drink.

I began to manipulate Tandice, to turn the conversation around.

"You know, sweetheart, I'm feeling really good," I said. "It was a smart idea to quit drinking when I did."

"Oh, I agree, Mom!" Tandice said, buying right into it.

It kills me, now, to remember this, but I was *leading* her into a dead end. I was being nice to her to get her close to me, and I was about to smash her. She was standing there, very blonde under the kitchen lights, waving a wooden spoon as she talked, and her eyes were so innocent. That's what I remember most. Her eyes.

"So I think I'll reward myself," I said casually, "and have one glass of wine."

And in that moment I saw her eyes turn from the childlike belief and love to absolute disgust. It was as though I could see everything I'd ever done mirrored in her eyes. It was the same look that Patt saw. Why? Why did I go ahead and pour myself a glass of wine (and later, another and another glass) when Tandice was looking at me as if I'd just crawled out from under a rock?

I've told this story often. Inevitably there's an outpouring of identity with it, with the pain, and with the fact that, for us, nothing will make that pain go away *except another drink*. At that point, you *must* alter your mind.

The point is that *in recovery*

Almost Any Amount of Damage to Relationships Can Be Repaired

But the alcoholic who is still drinking feels no hope. Alcoholism is a disease of hopelessness. If experiences like the one I had with my daughter — where the feelings of pain are so intense — do not drive an alcoholic into sobriety, what does?

What is a "bottom"?

It is that point at which one is literally hammered into suicide, or some form of death, or surrender. And the surrender need not be walking into a support group meeting but the

Admission of Defeat

This is the admission, "I need help." It's that simple.

When people go from describing how they hit bottom to how they took the next step, it always comes out as, "I asked for help." In my case, it was picking up the phone and calling information for help. In Patt's case, there was an Alano club in the small town in which she lived. She simply walked down the block and walked in. Some people look in the Yellow Pages and start calling hospitals.

Many times at a meeting, you'll hear that moment of hitting bottom described as "I prayed to God," followed by a long, involved story that varies widely in content: "Two minutes later, my next door neighbor came over to borrow the lawnmower, and he turned out to be a recovering alcoholic," sort of story, but it always centers on asking for help.

So hitting bottom is a series of three actual steps.

1. Admitting defeat or surrender.
2. Asking for help.
3. Taking a step of action.

It doesn't matter what the details of the story are. What matters is that whatever action step is taken, it is always

A Step of Surrender

And it seems to have to be an articulated surrender — a surrender in which we admit to someone that we've lost control over our drinking — whether it's in a meeting, or in a hospital, or we fall on our knees and pray out loud to God. It's *out* now. It's

No Longer Just in Our Head

To recover, both the alcoholic and the people close to the alcoholic need to be truthful — to be aware of what the truth is. And the alcoholic, as we've seen throughout this book, doesn't *know* what the truth is. Like the martyred spouse of an adulterer, we are usually "the last to know."

Today, there is so much more help available, for both the alcoholic and her family, than there was when Patt hit bottom fifteen years ago. ("There were," she remembers, "hardly any women in AA then. Now the numbers seem about equal, with more women coming in all the time.") In Terry's case, the bottom was raised for her by the compassionate intervention of her employer.

Help to put us on the road to recovery can come in many forms. Most important is that we reach an awareness that our juggling acts are no longer working — that we're the only ones being fooled. With such insight, we can see that we need help. This help continues to be available as we move through the challenges of recovery. Using resources, being realistic in work and personal commitments, managing the dual stress of multiple roles, and setting realistic recovery goals are all important. Maintaining balance in these important tasks facilitates recovery. Progress, not perfection, in recovery allows us to be truly happy, joyous, and free.

CHAPTER TEN

Spiritual Recovery: Healing the Run in the Soul

I had a plan to get out of my situation. I'd had that plan for about four years, and that was suicide.
— My own words,
spoken in recovery,
at a meeting

* * *

It's 2:00 A.M. and quiet inside my condominium. All the blinds are pulled down. The doors are bolted. They've been bolted for the past three weeks, and for three weeks I haven't changed my clothes or washed my hair. I can't remember the last time I ate. I've been existing — if "existing" is the right word — on alcohol, cocaine, and crystal.

My body is just skin and bone now. Hanging loosely on it is a stained, rag-like garment. When I first put it on three weeks earlier, it was a peach silk designer nightgown. The stale smell of spilled beer rises from the carpet as I sit on the edge of my king-sized bed staring down at the gun in my hand.

Maybe I should call somebody to say good-bye?

Who? I don't have any friends left.

I've been keeping my daughters at a distance, terrified that they'll see me like this. I've lied to my co-workers in the art business. They think my father has died and I'm in New Mexico.

The only human being I've seen in three weeks is Alan, my pusher. We have a "relationship," Alan and I, and I believe that he cares about me. The fumbling, unsatisfying sex that happens when we tumble into bed together has at least given me moments of relief from fear. From guilt. But Alan is as sick as I am. And, deep down, I sense that he's not capable of worrying about me.

The only person in the world, I decide, that I really want to say good-bye to is my father's warmhearted second wife, my stepmother, Betty.

When I reach her, she sounds sleepy.

"I love you, Betty," I mumble.

"Ann Ruth? Is that you?" Her voice is soft, very southern. "Ann Ruth, it's three in the morning here in Santa Fe."

The drugs I've taken are coursing through my bloodstream. I tell Betty that I'm going to kill myself in a few minutes because my life is unbearable. As she begins to sound alarmed, I hang up.

The gun, a small derringer, was made specially for me by a gunsmith I had met four years earlier. I dated him for the sole reason that I needed a gun for my suicide plan. I had talked and charmed and seduced him into doing it.

Where shall I point it?

In my mouth?

But what if the shot doesn't kill me? What if I wake up in a hospital, horribly mutilated?

Perhaps in the ear? Straight through the brain. . . .

I can't lift the gun out of my lap.

I can't live! I'm overwhelmed by the pain, by the eternal juggling act an addict exists with. I've lied to the point where I can't lie anymore.

If I can't live and I can't die, I'm trapped. There's no place to go.

I sit on the edge of my bed, feeling paralyzed, for hours. Gradually morning light begins to seep in under the wooden blinds. My eyes, half-closed under swollen lids, focus on a ribbon of sunlight. As I stare at it, the light seems to move, to be alive, to be forming words. Somewhere inside my head, very clearly, I hear the same words that are forming on the windowsill: "Call AA."

Is it the effect of all those drugs? A spiritual experience? I'm too desperate to even try to figure it out. I can't see well enough to use a phone book, so I get a number from information. A man who says his name is Chas answers.

"Do you have a problem with alcohol?" he asks.

"Maybe. . . ."

Chas asks for my number. "I'm going to call around and find somebody to call you back," he explains, and hangs up.

And the pain is excruciating.

It's been six hours since I've taken anything. My teeth are beginning to chatter. I huddle, shivering in my stained nightgown, gripped by terror, by loneliness, by isolation.

At twenty minutes to nine, I received what I now know was a Twelfth Step call. A woman, who said her name was Mary M., called to find out where I lived.

She says she will be right over, so I creep downstairs to wait for her.

As I reach the bottom stair, the doorbell peals. Help is here! So quickly! I pull open the door and look straight into the muzzle of a huge black pistol. It's held by a highway patrolman. Over his shoulder, I can see three police cars, "bubble gum" lights flashing, parked by the curb. Neighbors are milling on the sidewalk. Crouching behind the tree on my front lawn are two more police officers, aiming riot guns.

My stepmother has called the police. She's warned them that I'm suicidal, on drugs, and have a gun. Those men are prepared for anything.

"Step outside," the policeman snaps.

I've gone too far, I think. *This time, I'm not going to be able to talk, or charm, or seduce my way out of trouble. This time, I'm going to jail.*

The tap dance is over.

I stare helplessly at the policeman. He stares back. A flicker of uncertainty crosses his face. He can see I'm not armed. It's obvious I'm not hiding any lethal weapons; I'm almost nude. He looks as if he's not sure what to do about me.

Out in the street, a car door slams. A large woman with blue-rinsed white hair — a dowager duchess of a woman — is striding up my walkway. I watch in amazement as she cuts through the crowd of neighbors, as she sweeps, unfazed, past the men with the riot guns. She reminds me of an ocean liner!

She is Mary.

"I'll take care of her," she tells the policeman on my door-step, to his obvious relief. I'm beginning to shiver again, violently. My legs feel too weak to hold me up. My stomach is lurching with dry heaves. Mary-the-duchess draws me inside, wraps me in a blanket.

I huddle on the sofa as she makes me hot tea with honey.

"Do you think you're an alcoholic?" she asks.

Even in the middle of this humiliating defeat, some of my old arrogance still rises. "Well, perhaps," I say cautiously.

Then Mary, this dignified blue-haired lady, sits down beside me and tells me of her own turning point — of waking up in a seedy hotel room in Europe with no idea of where she was, or who the man who had just left the bed was. And as she talks, I recognize some of the places she's telling me about. She and I must have danced on some of the same tables!

* * *

I surrendered that morning, although I didn't realize it at the time.

When I admitted to Mary that I was an alcoholic, it was the first time I had admitted it. Even to myself.

The progression of this disease is so insidious. There were so many times — at least in the early years — when I didn't have a hangover, or wasn't embarrassing myself, or wasn't throwing up in some stranger's bathroom. Most of the time, I was able to think of myself as a successful career woman with a loving husband and fantastic children.

But I did see myself as a woman who had numerous problems, who needed alcohol to stay sane. As, little by little, my life fell apart, I clung to the idea of alcohol and drugs as an antidote to my problems, rather than as the cause of them. I felt that *any* woman who had my problems would drink!

That first sober morning — it was the first day of June — as my body began to detoxify, I was just beginning to face life in the real world. I knew, intuitively, that it would be dangerous for me to go to a hospital. In a hospital, even as beaten down as I was, I would rally into my grandiose "Queen Ann" act and manipulate a nurse or a doctor into giving me drugs.

So Mary stayed with me that entire day. While I huddled, alternately burning and freezing, beside her on the sofa, she shared her experience, strength, and hope. At some point, she must also have called my older daughter Deanna because the next morning Deanna arrived to get me ready for my first meeting.

I was so weak that she had to hold me up in the shower while she shampooed my hair. It took me an hour to put on some makeup. (My hands were shaking so hard that twice I jabbed myself in the eye with the mascara brush.) But I can remember exactly what I wore to that first meeting. Designer jeans. A navy blue cashmere sweater. And, under the sweater, a crisp white shirt with a collar. The "preppie" look. Because, I figured, no one would think that a woman dressed like this could possibly be as dirty as I felt I was inside.

I was terrified when Mary ushered me in. I felt humiliated. But to my amazement, I felt at home there — safe for perhaps the first time in my life. In spite of my circumstances, I began to feel there was hope.

After a while, I realized that there was a common thread of some kind of spiritual awakening or awareness running through almost every turning-point story I heard. It happened to us alcoholics as we hit bottom.

✳   ✳   ✳

Leah, thirty-eight, is a nurse in an intensive care unit. She says:

> *Until I was in my early thirties, I didn't believe in God. My grandparents were pillars of their church, but at home they were bastards. Their church was very bigoted, very rigid. It preached fire and brimstone. I always felt that if there was a God, He wouldn't let little children be hurt and scared and sexually abused like I had been.*
>
> *For most of my life, I didn't believe I was an alcoholic either. Then, six years ago, my boyfriend got into legal trouble, and he was ordered by a judge to go to AA. I* thought, I'm a nurse. I need to understand these people. I'll go with him.
>
> *They had a woman speaker that night. A professional woman. I was fascinated by the fact that she was up there admitting she was a drunk. Then she started to describe her denial system.*
>
> *I thought,* She's describing me!
>
> *All those nights when I'd cruised the bars and I thought I was being so liberated, I was really acting out the sexual abuse of my past. I was hunting for men I could control.*
>
> *Gradually, as she talked, the rest of the room disappeared. She grew clearer and clearer to me. It was as if she was in a white spotlight. She was speaking to me alone.*
>
> *We were alone!*
>
> *I thought* Oh, my God . . . Oh, my God . . . I am an alcoholic! I'm just like my mother!
>
> *That night was incredible. I know it was a spiritual experience. It's difficult to describe, but, yes, there is an energy. A force for good. A God.*

* * *

After I got into a Twelve Step program and began listening to the stories of other recovering alcoholics, I came to think of my experience with the light under the blinds as a spiritual one. I heard so many similar experiences described.

It didn't seem to matter what religious background we came from — or even if we had *any* religious background. As I listened to others in the program, I realized that the comfort of turning one's life over to a Higher Power — whatever you perceived that Higher Power to be — was essential to recovery.

This awareness was strengthened by a series of incidents that happened to me in early recovery.

When I first got sober, I still had a lot of drugs in the house, including some cocaine hidden inside my jewelry box. I remember thinking, *I had better save this in case the program doesn't work.*

On my seventeenth sober morning, I woke up at 3:00 A.M. and stared at the dresser drawer where the cocaine was hidden. It was as though I had X-ray vision. I could feel, literally, waves of heat pulsing from the drawer. It terrified me. I thought, *I must get rid of this!*

I grabbed it from the drawer and, moving faster than I've ever moved in my life, I ran to the bathroom and flushed it down the toilet.

At that moment, I realized I was safe. I didn't want a backup. At that moment, I accepted the Twelve Step program, I accepted sobriety, and I accepted the gift of a Higher Power. Fear had been replaced by faith.

A couple weeks later, I shared this experience at a meeting in an Alano Club. After I had finished speaking, a big, athletic-looking young woman in a black leather jacket came up to me.

"My name's Sally. Tell me more about flushing the cocaine," she said.

"Er . . . what do you want to know, Sally?"

"I've got some," she said. From out of her bulging black leather shoulder bag, she pulled a plastic-wrapped package of white powder. I peered down at it. Good grief, she had at least half a kilo there!

"I came to the meeting tonight to make up my mind," she explained. "If you can do it, I can. Come to the rest room with me."

"You have so much of it," I muttered nervously, as I followed her into the ladies room. "I mean, mine was just a little bit. Are you a dealer?"

Sally said that she was. In fact, she shared a house with several roommates, all dealers, who sounded as though they were involved in big-time crime. The cocaine belonged to them! Visions of hit-men clutching Uzis flashed through my mind. What was I getting into?

At that point, though, I was trapped in the power of my own story. And, looking back, I know that I had come to trust the program.

"Shall I flush it?" Sally asked.

We poured it down together. As Sally pulled the lever, I stared at the white powder swirling down the drain. What if it got stuck? What if we had stopped up a toilet with cocaine at an Alano Club?

It disappeared with a gurgle.

All that money!

"Now what?" Sally said. She was looking at me expectantly. I was only thirty-three days sober! What did I know?

"We could say the Third Step prayer together?" I suggested. After I had begun to go to the meetings, that prayer had been one of the first things I clung to. So, standing there in the bathroom, Sally and I said:

"God, I offer myself to Thee — to build with me and to do with me as Thou wilt. Relieve me of the bondage of self, that I may better do Thy will. Take away my difficulties, that victory over them may bear witness to those I would help of Thy Power, Thy Love, and Thy Way of life. May I do Thy will always!"*

---

* From the Big Book, *Alcoholics Anonymous*, 3rd ed. (New York: A.A. World Services, Inc., 1976), 63.

"Now what?" Sally said. "Now I don't have a place to sleep."

We went downstairs to a pay phone. We called her room-mates and broke the news. They seemed to take it fairly well, but Sally obviously wouldn't be welcomed back with open arms. I didn't feel strong enough to take her home with me. (I still had three-weeks-worth of beer cans and unwashed glasses rolling about under my bed. Because of their smell, I was afraid to touch them.)

I went out into the Alano Club restaurant and said, "Sally needs a place to sleep." And, of course, another recovering alcoholic — one with a lot more sobriety than I had — volunteered to take her home.

These kinds of things happened to me a lot in the early days, and it helped me to know that I belonged. I came to believe that God was working through me. I was over-whelmed with the power of the program.

❈   ❈   ❈

Mary, forty-two, a mental health counselor in a large hospital says:

> *The first time I sensed that there was a Power greater than myself was when I was seven-months sober, and my friend Chris and I went to a weekend retreat in Arizona. It was to be a sober adventure.*
>
> *When we go there, I was horrified to find the people there were everything I was afraid of. Nearly everyone was gay, and many of them were prostitutes or mental patients, and they were telling their stories in these in-credibly wide-open marathon meetings that went all the time. They went on all night by candlelight.*
>
> *All my defenses were up. I was on my high horse. I mean, I was a respectable therapist, one of the few people in my family who wasn't crazy. I wasn't like these people!*

"I want to go home," I told Chris.

"Please stay, Mary," she said. "I have a feeling there's something here for us."

Well, we'd come in her car. I went back to our room and started to read As Bill Sees It,[*] *and I opened the book at random to the passage that deals with running away because of fear.*

The next morning, I was assigned to lead a meeting with a man who was a mental patient. Up went my defenses again. I had to label him crazy, and me okay.

But that man was so kind to me. He was so compassionate. He touched my heart. By the end of the meeting, I was in tears. Sobbing. As my defenses started to crumble, I realized that he, and all the others, were all just humans. Like me, they were trying to get well. I couldn't fool myself any longer. Maybe I wasn't a paid prostitute, but I'd done just as many degrading things.

I felt a sense of compassion for everyone there, including me. Then I began to feel euphoric.

It was sunset as Chris and I began our drive home. I looked out of the car windows, and the desert landscape appeared to be vibrating! The rocks, the trees — everything seemed to throb with sunlight. It was beautiful.

I had always lived in such a dreary, threatening world. This world was a miracle. And I was a part of it.

Recovery for me, like Mary and Sally and Leah, is definitely a spiritual experience.

I went into sobriety feeling so small and worthless. I was sure that the degradation I felt inside must somehow show on the outside too. I was afraid of everything, but most of all I feared rejection.

The love I experienced in the program — after so many years of isolation, of lying and cheating, and of manipulating

---

[*] *As Bill Sees It*, published by A.A. World Services, Inc., New York, N. Y., 1985.

others — was indescribable. I went to meetings three or four times a day at first.

The program heals so many things when we learn acceptance. When people accept you unconditionally, you begin to feel self-esteem. You begin to care about yourself. The fellowship members loved me when I felt totally unlovable and could not love myself.

And the spiritual part of recovery, as Mary discovered when she looked out of the car window in Arizona, is the part that makes things beautiful. *Really* beautiful. It made me notice how delicious ice cream tasted, or the jewel-like colors of a stained glass window, or how clearly the stars shine at night.

It's astonishing. Like a very small child, I began to really experience the scents, colors, and flavors of the life around me.

This disease of alcoholism, with its symptoms of loneliness and denial, is a disease of the spirit as well as the body. It deadens us.

It leaves scars on our souls.

How are they healed?

An easy visual image is to think of yourself, as you were when trapped by addiction, as a cup filled with fear. Then, in recovery, little by little, you empty the fear from the cup.

You refill it the same way — slowly, drop by drop — with faith. *And you can draw that faith through the faith, the strength of others.*

Fear and Faith Cannot Exist in the Same Heart

Dick, a friend of mine in the program is short and round. His hair has turned prematurely grey. He tells a story of riding his motorcycle back from a long trip and pulling into a service station to get gas.

Suddenly he found himself surrounded by a motorcycle gang. A *tough-looking* motorcycle gang. Ripped-out sleeves. Huge boots. Evil-looking tattoos. Chains.

As they loomed around him, sneering, one of them made a remark obviously intended to intimidate him. Dick looked him in the eye and said, "You know, I'm an alcoholic, and I don't drink anymore. I've known terror and pain you wouldn't believe. I've looked the devil straight in the eye, and, feller, you don't show me nothin'."

They roared off on their bikes and left Dick alone with his faith.

Your spirituality is a unique and personal thing. I agree with the expression, heard often by people in a Twelve Step program: "Find a God you can do business with." That beautiful sense of inner peace, the peace that makes you feel almost inviolate, comes when you find a spirituality that works for *you.*

A crucial step toward developing your spirituality is looking back at your own experiences with religion — or the lack of them — in the past.

* * *

I believed in God when I was a child. Later, when I was a rebellious eighteen, religion seemed weak. Religious people seemed weak. I felt I didn't need God. I was an actress. I was going to take on the world!
— CONNIE, seventy-two

* * *

What did God mean to *you* while you were growing up?

The spirit of love? Did you feel God as a loving presence always with you? Or in your family, was religion used to control, to threaten and punish? ("The wicked will burn in Hell" sort of thing, with "wicked" applied to everything from wearing makeup to being an unwed mother?)

Think back.

Did you go to Sunday school? Did you enjoy it? Or were you, like me, bored by Sunday school to the point of sitting there and unravelling the lace from the tops of your socks?

I have always believed in God. Yet, by the time I was a young wife, going to church had become, like everything else, a part of "looking good." It was one more thing to do, one more item on the agenda of my eternal tap dance. I was a member of the Altar Guild for years, arranging flowers and carrying casseroles to church suppers.

Every Sunday, I went to church, towing along my beautifully dressed children, because it was what "we" all did. I found no comfort in religion, no peace or serenity in those services. I don't think this was the fault of the church. I was too tightly bound in the cocoon of my own conflicts to be open to God. My thoughts were always on my problems, not spiritual matters.

This is not the experience of all alcoholic women, but it is for many of us and for our partners too. David, my first husband, usually refused to go to church at all. I would feel compelled to make excuses for him. He was working. He was tired. He was painting the house.

For me, Sunday just meant more stress, more lies, and more hypocrisy.

* * *

In recovery, return to spirituality was a gradual thing. There were no lights flashing. No celestial bursts of music as I stood in a doorway. Being a person who loves drama, I would have liked it to be that way. When I was drinking, I had cut off all my feelings. They were too painful. Then one day, when I'd been sober for about a year, I was visiting my daughter. I was walking in the pine forest alone, saying the Third Step prayer, and I realized I was "inside happy."

— CONNIE, seventy-two

* * *

A helpful technique to use in early recovery can be writing an ongoing letter to God. A private letter, just between you and your Higher Power.

✳ ✳ ✳

It's 9:00 P.M., a rainy evening in September. The heels of Terry's boots click against the wet tarmac of the YMCA parking lot as she hurries to her car. She feels excited. She has just heard a woman at tonight's meeting talk about writing a letter to God. A letter to God! The woman's words are echoing in her head. Terry feels an urgent need to try it herself.

Her car feels cold as she slides into the front seat. The smell of the dog still lingers from last Saturday's trip to the vet. She really must get by the car wash tomorrow, if there's time. There's never enough time. How had she ever managed to find all that time to drink?

In the light from the nearby mercury vapor street lamp, she rummages through her purse. No notebook! No pen! Good grief, *she thinks,* I'm a journalist running around without a notebook or a pen. *She does have the envelope from her gas and electric bill, though, and a very sharp eyeliner pencil. Forest Green. In the shadowed front seat of her chilly car, Terry smiles.* God, surely, won't mind being written to in Forest Green? *She prints carefully:*

> DEAR GOD,
>   I'LL RE-DO THIS PROPERLY AS SOON AS I GET HOME, BUT RIGHT THIS MINUTE I WANT TO GET SOMETHING DOWN. THIS EVENING, I HEARD A WOMAN TALKING ABOUT HOW SHE WRITES TO YOU EVERY NIGHT.
>   SHE LOOKED SO HAPPY, SO GLOWING. SHE SEEMED SO AT PEACE WITH HERSELF. SHE SAID THAT SHE HAD ASKED YOUR HELP IN HEALING HER SPIRIT, IN HEALING THE SCARS SHE HAD INSIDE.
>   PLEASE HELP ME, GOD. I FEEL SUCH A NEED FOR GUIDANCE, SUCH A NEED TO HEAL MY SPIRIT. . . .

* * *

Many times, after a meeting, I've noticed someone scribbling frantically on an old envelope, or on the back of his or her checkbook. Things that you hear other recovering people say often "hit" you in early sobriety. They can be very simple things. They usually are! But to a newly recovering alcoholic, they can feel like a revelation — as though you've been struck by a lightning bolt.

I remember one evening after a meeting. I was having trouble writing out my Fourth Step — the Step in which you take an inventory of yourself — and I was standing outside, talking about this to a man named Ergo who had many years of sobriety.

Ergo began telling me a long, long story about faith. *Gosh, this is boring,* I thought, standing there shifting my weight from hip to hip and trying to look interested. My mind began to wander. *Is there any milk in the house for breakfast? Maybe I'd better dash into the 7-11 on my way home. Do I have any money with me?*

And then he said one little thing.

I can't now recall his exact words, although it was one of those "clichés" of the program. Something about getting to the edge of a cliff of faith, and jumping off. But, suddenly — pow! — I was hit with a tremendous insight. It was the answer I needed!

I took off so fast that I didn't even stop to say good-bye to the poor man. (Later I imagined him muttering, "She was just here a second ago. Where did she go?") It seemed vitally important to get home as quickly as possible, to work on my Fourth Step. I drove home feeling intensely excited, his words echoing in my head.

This is really what growth in the program is. It's a continuous process of opening yourself up.

In sobriety, we need to make peace with any religious experiences of the past that may have caused us anger or resentment. Newcomers try many paths. Some will go to

church. Others will cross the street to avoid being near one.
But all of us who are more than a little sober will make peace
with God or with our perception of a Higher Power.

Whatever path you choose, begin now, for it is the key to
the serenity that can bring you so much joy in your future.

* * *

How can someone who loves an alcoholic woman help her
to hit bottom sooner, help to spare her from more damage? Or,
if she is already in recovery, how can you give her the support
she needs while still taking care of your own well-being?

The next chapter, "In This Together: To the Men Who Love
Us," focuses on answers to both these questions. (If you are a
recovering woman, you may want to give it to the man in your
life to read, along with an encouraging hug.) Although it was
written to the man who is married to, or who dates or lives
with, an alcoholic woman, the next chapter is really for everyone — from her boss to her son to her grandfather.

It is for anyone who cares about her survival.

CHAPTER ELEVEN

In This Together:
To the Men Who Love Us

> *I missed the romantic touches that were tied in with alcohol — the champagne we used to drink in bed once in awhile — the dinners with candlelight and wine. The first time in Sue's recovery that we went out to dinner I said, "Do you mind if I have a drink?" Sue said she didn't mind. But it felt weird. I felt uncomfortable having that one drink by myself.*
>
> — BOB
> Married for eighteen years
> to Sue, who has been in
> recovery for eleven years

* * *

In a church basement with walls papered with children's drawings of happy-face pumpkins, Jeff sits in a circle of fifteen women and three men.

It's his first Al-Anon meeting.

What am I doing here? he thinks as a plump woman wearing a Hawaiian *muumuu* starts to tell her story. Her husband, she explains, has relapsed. After eight months in his recovery, he's gone back to the bars.

"I woke up at two o'clock this morning, and he was going through my handbag," she says. "I snatched it from him and said

169

'Jim, don't! We're already behind with the rent.' And he hit me across the side of my head."

Jeff's mind whirls. Jesus! That poor woman. He can see her blackened eye through the heavy makeup she's wearing. Why does she stay with this guy? And what does any of it have to do with his relationship with Terry? Terry doesn't live like this.

But she is an alcoholic. A recovering one, as both she and his Aunt Lindsay keep pointing out. His aunt! In his whole life he can never remember seeing her act like a drunken woman. She's another mystery to him.

This whole business of recovery is a mystery to him. He just knows that he feels confused by it. Sometimes he even feels jealous and threatened by it.

Like last Saturday. He had been at the mall with Terry because she was helping him pick out some lamps for his apartment. He always enjoyed being out in public with her. He felt proud of her. Terry turned so many heads.

They had been walking peacefully along, holding hands, keeping an eye on Beth and Cody who were several yards ahead. Suddenly a young guy in a gray jogging suit stepped out of a shop, The Coffee Grinders, right in front of them.

"Terry!" the guy shouted.

"Ron!" Terry cried.

As Jeff had stood there watching, Ron had flung his arms around Terry and hugged her. It had seemed to him to be an extremely long hug. They were beaming at each other. Terry was glowing, looking at this guy as if he were her long-lost twin or something! It had made him feel strangely left out. Like the Invisible Man.

"Who was that guy?" he had asked her, as soon as Ron's jogging-suited body had loped off toward the nearest escalator.

"Ron?" Terry said. "I hardly know him. But I see him at meetings all the time."

Sometimes Jeff has the distinct feeling that he would get more attention from Terry if he were a recovering alcoholic.

In the pumpkin-decorated church basement, the woman in the muumuu is being replaced as a speaker by a man named Mitch. Mitch appears to Jeff to be about his own age, a big, blond-bearded ophthalmologist. His wife Kate has been in recovery for nine years.

170

Nine years! Has the guy been coming to these meetings for nine years?

At first, Jeff only half listens to what Mitch is saying. He gathers that Mitch loves his wife. That he's proud of her. That Kate, the mother of five children, has recently graduated magna cum laude from somewhere.

Then Mitch says, "My 'normie' friends sometimes ask me why I've been coming to Al-Anon meetings for so many years. They think that surely, by now, I've learned all I need to know about alcoholism.

"But having my own Twelve Step program, as Kate has hers, has changed my life. It helps me to get things off my chest, to cope with stress. I'm more productive at work because of it. I'm a better father. Kate and I can share feelings now. We can talk the same language."

The same language.

Something — a glimpse of recognition — stirs inside Jeff. There have been several times lately when Terry and his aunt have been talking and, although they were speaking English, they could have been conversing in Russian for all the meaning he got from their conversation. A lot of the words they used seemed to be everyday words, but their definitions were different.

He looks at Mitch, at this sensible-sounding, solid man who reminds him a lot of Kirk Douglas in the movie The Vikings, *and he wonders if Mitch will have time to talk to him after the meeting.*

❊　❊　❊

My wife and I went to a party where everyone but me was a recovering alcoholic. All the conversation revolved around their experiences. I didn't have any of those kinds of stories to share. I managed to steer the talk round to world events, but five minutes later they were back to their experiences. I felt like a non-chess player at a chess championship. I couldn't contribute any great moves!
— RICHARD, fifty-one
Married for eight years to
Nanette, who has been in
recovery for five years

❊　❊　❊

The bond between recovering alcoholics is very special. As the Big Book says, we are like survivors of some terrible shipwreck who meet again on shore. We're alive! To us, sharing our stories means sharing our survival.

Even at a casual encounter, like that of Terry and Ron at the mall, it isn't just the joy of seeing one another that makes us hug with such enthusiasm. In our minds, it's the joy of knowing we've escaped disaster. That fond embrace communicates the bond, and the miracle of the fact that we're here — we didn't go down with the ship!

❊   ❊   ❊

When I was growing up in the fifties, I never saw anybody drunk. My parents kept a bottle of something in the china cabinet for company, and that was about it. When I was a teenager, I got drunk twice — this was on trips to Tijuana with friends — and both times I hated it. I never drank again.

— CARL
Married for three years to
Linda, who is currently in
a hospital treatment pro-
gram for the second time

❊   ❊   ❊

If alcoholism was never a part of your education, if you yourself are a social drinker or a non-drinker, loving an alcoholic woman can be pretty confusing. How could it be otherwise? In early recovery, *we* don't understand ourselves.

❊   ❊   ❊

After I'd dropped Nanette off at the hospital's recovery unit, I was in a fog. She was such a good actress that I hadn't known she was having a problem with cocaine. I felt . . . betrayed. There was this part of her life that had been secret to me. I was too disturbed to go to work, so I went to the zoo and just wandered around all day, like a robot.

— RICHARD

* * *

If you love a woman who has a drinking or substance problem, the best way to help her is

To Help Yourself

There you are — a human being with all the usual requirements for warmth, love, and appreciation. In the early stages of her recovery, however, she is probably going to be too preoccupied to give much thought to how you are feeling. (This will change, so hang on!)

In the early stages, you will be adjusting to the fact that she now seems to be constantly rushing off to meetings. ("Just fix yourself a cheese sandwich or something, Don — I have to go!") She may be spending hours on the phone, talking to people you've never heard of. She may be reading self-help books at midnight. And she may not be the wild, abandoned sex partner she used to be after three or four drinks.

If you are feeling, understandably, a bit neglected, if you are having difficulties accepting her recovery program

Find a Program for Yourself

How?

- *Educate yourself about the disease of alcoholism.* Learn all you can about alcoholism and the stages of the recovery process, through books, tapes, seminars, and so forth.
- *Get some support for yourself.* You need some attention! The Yellow Pages, your doctor, or your local library are all

sources from which to find a Twelve Step group such as Al-Anon, that feels friendly and comfortable to you. (Sometimes that means trying several different groups.) Even if you're not normally a joiner, you'll be strengthened by the encouragement, the warmth, and the insights that people in a Twelve Step group can share with you. Many Al-Anon groups have special meetings for newcomers.

- *Check all your options.* If you work for a large or mid-sized company, they may sponsor an Employee Assistance Program (EAP) to help employees with problems related to substance abuse.

❊ ❊ ❊

When I first went to Al-Anon, I couldn't relate to the stories. People talked about violent fights, going bankrupt, having to live with their children in a car. That wasn't us. But after a few months, I no longer listened to the stories but to people sharing their feelings. When they spoke about fear or anger or frustration I could relate to that. That's what tied me in. The stories were just what caused the feelings. The causes were different for everybody, but the feelings were the same.

— Bob
Married for eighteen years
to Sue, who has been in
recovery for eleven years

❊ ❊ ❊

We've been focusing on the husband/wife relationship. How about fathers? How does a father feel when he discovers that his daughter has a drinking problem?

My friend Tom is in his early sixties, with beautiful white hair and bright blue eyes crinkled by laugh lines. When Tom walks into a meeting, he always looks as if he would be more at home on a golf course.

Lori, his much-loved daughter, was a late baby — the first child of his second marriage. Both Tom and Lori's mother, who are now divorced, are recovering alcoholics.

Lori began drinking and using at the age of ten. By the time she was thirteen, both of her parents were recovering alcoholics, working a program.

"We realized she had a drinking problem," Tom said. "But, like a lot of parents, we didn't realize how serious it was." They had no idea, he added, that she was using so many drugs. As part of a completely different generation from their daughter, Tom and his wife had been addicted strictly to alcohol. Neither of them had ever used other drugs. They were totally unprepared for the extent of Lori's problem.

They knew they had to do something though. They began going to Al-Anon meetings. By this time, Lori was driving. One night, she smashed Tom's car into a neighbor's car, broke several bones, and ended up in the hospital. It was obvious that Lori had been drunk and out of control. The neighbor — looking extremely uneasy — came over to confront Tom.

This crisis turned out to be the leverage that Tom and his wife needed to get Lori into the program. While she was still feeling scared, shaken, and guilty, they insisted that she go to meetings. And, at the age of only seventeen, Lori "got" the program. At twenty-one (legally able to drink!), she had four years of sobriety. Now at twenty-five, eight years sober, she's in law school.

As Tom points out:

> *We were lucky. But even if she hadn't gotten the program then, the earlier you get into it, the earlier you get into* knowledge *of recovery.*
>
> *And the earlier you get into recovery, the less damage there is. I can look back at some of the humiliating, or dangerous, or sad alcohol-related experiences I've had and think,* Lori will be spared that.

What's Tom's advice to other parents? It echoes part of this chapter.

"Educate yourself," he stresses. "Find some support for yourself. We went to Al-Anon to get *clear* about our child's problem."

Tom also feels it's important for people (not just parents) to confront their own drinking and using. He's very fond of saying: "Example is not *a* way to teach. It's the *only* way.

Recovery from alcoholism, just like the disease itself,

Goes Through Predictable Stages

This is why people who have "been there before you" can be such a tremendous help. Education about recovery can help you to anticipate the stages and the emotional turmoil a recovering addict passes through — the highs, the lows, the euphoria, the depression, and fear.

As both of you grow, your relationship *will* get better. A lot better! In fact, like Mitch, the ophthalmologist Jeff heard speaking at a meeting, you may find that everything in your life has changed for the better.

* * *

I'd reached the point where I felt like all I wanted to do was crawl into bed and never wake up again. Today I wake up glad to be alive. I'm excited about the future.
— GARY
Married for twenty-nine
years to Sue, who has been
in recovery for four years

* * *

The following two stories are from men who found, from the self-examination that came while their wives were recovering, tools for coping with life's stresses in general.

Gary, who was previously quoted, is a partner in an adver-
tising agency and a recovering alcoholic himself. Bob, a me-
chanical engineer, is a "normie." (Normies are the sort of
people who can leave half a glass of wine sitting on a table, and
forget about it!) By coincidence, both of their wives have
careers and are named Sue.

GARY'S STORY

I've learned some important things in the program, one of which is that my wife is entitled to her
feelings. I used to tell her, "You shouldn't feel that
way."

We were married for twenty-five years before
we hit bottom together, after a very tense visit from
my mother and aunt. Sue always became aggressive
at a certain point in her drinking. Night after night,
we'd argue, fight, and slam doors until about 2:00
A.M. I thought I drank because I had all these horrible problems — my wife in particular!

"Your mother and aunt are driving me crazy,"
Sue said. "Tell them to leave."

"I can't do that. You shouldn't *feel* that way!" I
said. I went outside — it was always my style to
retreat from her anger — which made her even angrier — and turned the yard sprinklers on. Then I
got drunk, left the sprinklers on all night, and the
next morning the whole lower level of the house was
flooded.

"Gary, I hate to say this, but you're slipping," my
mother told me. "Your marriage is never going to
work as long as you drink this much."

Things grew worse. I had this feeling that we
were headed for a tragedy. Sue was so depressed
that she went to a psychiatrist. When she told me
the doctor thought we might both be alcoholic, that

we should both get some help, I remember having a tremendous sense of relief, a *"Now* I understand!" feeling.

I was self-employed, with no health insurance, so we went to our physician, and he told us all about alcoholism, and suggested AA. "I'll put you in touch with somebody who'll help you," he said. And when the "somebody" came to our door, he turned out to be a friend. I knew he didn't drink, but I'd had no idea he was in recovery.

The next day, Sue and I went to a meeting together. I surrendered right away, before Sue did. From the first meeting, I felt the love there. My early euphoria didn't last though. I bought into the myth that once you were sober, you'd live happily ever after behind a white-picket fence. By November, five months into our recovery, I was sober and depressed, and Sue had slipped and was drinking in secret. I can remember getting into bed beside her one night and smelling vodka and tonic. *Oh, maybe it's just tonic,* I thought.

In January, Sue was in a car accident, probably because she was drinking. In February, she had back surgery for a ruptured disk, and she became addicted to the drugs the doctor prescribed. This was a *really* difficult time for us. Sue's sobriety date is eleven months later than mine.

Now life is very different. I look forward to each day. By staying with the program, by continuing to work on my character defects, not only my marriage has improved, but also my relationship with my clients.

As well as meetings and the couples' retreats we go to together, I belong to a men's Step study group. It's small, just five or six of us. Early on, when the other men asked me, "How are you feeling?" I had no idea. So they gave me a list with 100 feelings on it, and I picked from it — "Um, I guess number six and number twenty-seven" — like a Chinese menu.

Acceptance is a major part of recovery for both of us. We've come to accept a lot of things. Ourselves. Our condition. We accept each other for who we are and what we are. We're a lot gentler with each other.

BOB'S STORY

I had no idea that my wife was an alcoholic until I walked in the door after work, and Sue said, "I'm going to a Twelve Step meeting."

I said, "Okay." I didn't know what else to say. I was stunned. After she left, I kept thinking, *An alcoholic? Am I responsible in some way?* My image of alcoholic women then was rather shady. Not *Sue!*

We'd been married about seven years and had a little boy. I thought we were happy. There had been signs that Sue had a problem — she became very negative at a certain stage when she drank — and I used to tease her about her terrible hangovers — but I didn't connect this with alcoholism. Both of us were people-pleasers. We rarely even argued.

I walked on eggshells for a week and a half, and then Sue asked, "Would you like to come to a meeting, Bob?"

In my first meeting, I sat listening to all these horror stories. They didn't seem to have any connection to us. I must have had an expression of bewilderment on my face because a woman named Elaine came up and told me about support group meetings for family and friends. I began to go to them regularly. For the first few months, I was absorbed in trying to find out *why*.

Then I gradually began to feel resentment. Most of our friends drank. Our social activities had tapered off to nothing.

"I can't go to parties right now," Sue told me. "I can't be around people who drink."

I felt cheated. Angry. I didn't tell her how I felt though. One of my major character defects — as I've discovered since I've been working a program — was stuffing my feelings. I was brought up this way. A man takes care of his family. A man makes the money. I would stuff anything rather than hurt her.

Eleven months into recovery, Sue had a relapse. We were having an argument and she shouted, "I'm going out drinking! Come or stay!"

I went. At the Black Angus restaurant, we sat at a table on the edge of the dance floor, and Sue got bombed to the point where she could hardly walk.

When we got home, she was violently ill. Shivering. Cold. She couldn't stop shaking. We got into bed and I held her in my arms. After a couple of hours, she fell asleep.

That was it! That was ten years ago and she hasn't had a drink since then. She went to law school and is now a busy attorney. We've had more fights in recovery than we ever did before, but they're *quality* fights. We're honest about our feelings now.

The last few years in Al-Anon have been, for me, an ongoing discovery. It lets me see a picture of myself I never knew existed. It's neat because you don't reach a point where you say, "I can stop here because I've learned enough." I continue to learn. It's exciting!

But what if the woman in your life *isn't* in recovery yet? What if you've tried everything you can think of, and you're feeling desperate? How can you spare both of you a lot of pain by helping her to hit an earlier bottom?

Can you in effect raise the bottom?

Yes!

Anyone who is involved in any way with someone who has a problem can help by

Speaking the Truth, Whether She Listens or Not

You can help her by not covering up for her. By refusing to pick up the pieces for her.

Many people who live with alcoholics invent stories to shield their alcoholic partners from the consequences of drinking. ("Cindy had an allergic reaction to something the dentist gave her, Mom. *That's* why she was acting so strangely at your anniversary party.")

This, of course, enables the alcoholic to

Keep the Secret

But what happens to you — the person doing all the enabling? The most likely thing to happen to you will be that you'll build up a seething resentment toward the alcoholic. This usually explodes — wham! out of the blue! — in the face of the alcoholic, who then justifiably says something like, "Well, what the hell's wrong with *you?* What are you yelling at me for? All I did was drop a coffee cup."

Your "unjust" anger will simply give her another excuse to drink.

Telling the truth should include *all* alcoholics you know. The friend or co-worker who, after drinking four glasses of wine at lunch, drives you erratically back to the office. The sister-in-law who offers to baby-sit for you and then passes out on the sofa at 4:00 P.M.

Will you anger her if you tell her the truth about how her drinking makes you feel? How it puts you in jeopardy? Will you lose her as a friend, alienate her?

There's a possibility that you will.

I once stopped dating a man I was very attracted to because, one Sunday morning when we were having a quiet brunch, he smiled at me across the top of the newspaper he was reading and said, "Ann, you're so sweet, so nice when you don't drink. Drinking makes you a whole different person."

I was horrified. I felt that, somehow, he could see on the outside, all the dirtiness I felt on the inside. This man knew my secret! I never wanted to see him again.

Today if I knew where he was, I'd like to say to him, "Thank-you for telling me the truth."

I can count on the fingers of one hand the number of times anyone told me the truth about my drinking during my twenty years of alcoholism.

But what if *most* of the people an alcoholic woman knows begin telling her the truth? What if twenty people confront her — as Gary's mother did with him when he left the sprinklers on all night and flooded the house? We can't rationalize all these incidents away as we can when it's only one person. Twenty people know our secret!

The rules of polite society don't apply when someone's life is at stake.

If you saw a man having a heart attack in the middle of a public street, gasping, turning blue, you probably wouldn't stand around murmuring to everyone who passed, "Say, do you think it would insult him if I loosened his tie? Would he take offense if I called an ambulance?"

The point is that alcoholism is

A Deadly Disease

It's not a condition of morality, it's

Life and Death

So, if we see alcoholism for what it is, we'll begin to think, *Her life is at stake; therefore, I'm going to act as if this is a medical emergency.*

You may say, "Well, gosh, I can't just walk up to her and say 'You're an alcoholic.'" Of course you can't.

And, for you, that's not really the truth.

The truth for you is that this person's drinking is damaging to you in some way, and you can find a respectful way of communicating this to her. There's no need to hit her over the head with a machete. (Remember how Terry, in Chapter Nine, was confronted in the office of her general manager? He began by saying, "Terry, you've been a very valuable employee. . . ." Nobody was being harsh to her. Nobody was being rude.)

Presenting reality in palatable ways to the alcoholic woman means to point out to her *how her behavior is affecting you*. It's not up to you to judge her. It's up to you to tell her the truth.

Facing reality takes courage. This, as I'm sure you've noticed, is not for wimps! It requires courage to take on the challenges of living with a woman in early recovery.

You *are* going to find some aspects of it a stimulating adventure, though. So many alcoholic women are perfectionists who stuff down their real personalities as they struggle to be Wonderwoman. The inconveniences of early recovery are the price you pay for

Having a Real Person
Having Real Love

She is like someone who has been away for years, held as a hostage — a hostage to alcohol and chemicals. Now, she will be finding out who she really is. And that can be exciting for you.

If you want to feel really encouraged, go to some "open" meetings (Twelve Step meetings open to everyone) and talk to women who have been in recovery and working a program for several years. You'll find women who are living their lives with honesty and integrity. Women who are "pure gold."

You can see *yourself* differently too. In early recovery, instead of seeing yourself as the recipient of all her love and attention, see yourself as a tower of strength. In this situation, you are a knight in shining armor.

* * *

What would I say to a man who is married to a recovering alcoholic? Just love her and support her.
— RICHARD

CHAPTER TWELVE

Recovery:
What Women Need

*After I quit drinking, I didn't think there was going
to be any fun in my life again — ever. I figured I would
just keep going and endure.*
— DANIELLE, thirty-one

❋ ❋ ❋

*"But Neil, don't you feel guilty sometimes?" Terry is asking the
newspaper's food critic. "You get all those free meals, and then you
write that somebody's sauce tastes like wallpaper glue!"*

*Her cheeks feel flushed. The rose-colored fabric of her new dress
feels soft, sensuous, against her skin. All around her, under the
hanging stained glass lamps of Papa Luigi's Pasta Emporium, two
dozen of her co-workers are throwing a party for the "Viewpoint"
editor, Margaret, who is quitting to go to graduate school.*

*"Guilty! Never! Not if they're murdering good food," Neil says
indignantly. "I'll tell you, Terry, the worst, the absolute worst
experience of my life was in a restaurant called The Blue Grotto...."*

This, *Terry thinks*, is the first time I've gone to a party with
a group of non-recovering people since I hit bottom. I'm
really enjoying it.

*Beside her, Neil is raising his glass of red wine to his lips.
Suddenly he pauses. "Er... Terry, I just remembered. You know,
about your, um... does my drinking wine bother you?"*

"No. Not in the least. It's like licorice."

"Licorice?"

"Yes. I never liked it as a kid. So, of course, it wasn't part of my life. Now, when I see somebody enjoying alcohol, I feel the same way I would if I saw someone eating licorice. It's fine for them. But not for me."

"Ah . . . ," Neil murmurs. "You know, you've changed a lot, Terry. I like the new you."

"Your Osso Bucco Milanese, Signora." One of Papa Luigi's four sons, his face beaming with admiration for her, is sliding a veal dish she loves in front of her. She can smell the fragrance of herbs rising to join all the other peppery Italian country aromas filling the restaurant air.

It feels so good to be alive!

So good just to feel!

And these are her own feelings. They're not artificially created. Nobody has told her to feel this way. She's created her sobriety through working the Steps, through willingness and openness. Through honesty.

A tremendous feeling of power, of sheer happiness, washes through her. I feel high, high on life, she thinks.

"How's the boyfriend?" David is asking her. "What's his name? Jeff?"

Jeff! She hasn't even thought about Jeff in the last twenty-four hours.

"He's fine," she says. "Working pretty hard."

An image of another restaurant on another evening — of her first date with Jeff — flashes suddenly into Terry's mind. That band, the Pineapple Nights. The waitress in the wraparound mini-skirt who had made her feel so insecure. God, that terrible evening! And it could have been fun if she hadn't spent all her energy struggling to be whatever Jeff seemed to want her to be.

After that evening, she had been obsessed with thoughts about him. Would they get married? Would it work? Now, when Jeff keeps suggesting marriage at the rate of about once a week, it's . . . well, it's not that she doesn't care about him. She does plan to go on seeing him. Other things just seem so much more important.

Her number one priority now is the kids. She wants Beth and Cody to get to know her as a sober mother. She needs to create a new relationship with her parents too. Then there's her career. Like Margaret, she wants to go to graduate school.

Now isn't the time to take on a new husband.

But it's an exciting time. I've a sense of ease about my life now, *Terry thinks.* It's something I never expected to find. It's wonderful!

She feels a hand touch her arm. Jean, from personnel, is standing behind her chair.

"Terry, I just had to come over and tell you how terrific you're looking tonight," *she says.* "You're glowing like a thousand-watt bulb!" *Her eyes meet Terry's.* "I'm so glad to see you looking so good," *Jean says softly.*

❊ ❊ ❊

For much of my life, until I hit bottom I equated drinking with having fun. With glamour. With adventure.

After about two days of not drinking, even though I was hooked on the "miracle of sobriety," I was convinced that there was never going to be any fun in my life again. No joy. No pleasure. Nothing but grayness. The rest of my life was obviously going to be a dreary one. I'd just have to struggle through it, somehow.

My mind was still a very sick one.

Well, I thought, *if I'm going to be sentenced to this life of punishment, I had better find someone to marry, so at least I won't be lonely in my dreariness. Someone who doesn't drink, so I won't have a lot of temptation around. Maybe I should marry someone older? Then I won't have to live with him too long because he might die.*

The insanity of alcoholic thinking!

In my first month of sobriety, I was afraid that if I went out socially, people were going to force alcohol on me. I had been sober about three weeks when I was invited to a wedding.

I was very nervous about going. All that week I rehearsed and rehearsed what I was going to say when somebody offered me a drink. My sponsor had suggested that a simple, "No, thank-you," would be fine. But I worried that that wouldn't be enough.

I had a comedy version. "No, thank-you. I've had enough. Ha! Ha! Enough for the rest of my life." Then there was the "practicing rigorous honesty" version of "no, thank-you, I'm an alcoholic."

And nobody asked me!

There were waiters at the wedding, walking around with glasses on trays, but none of them came near me. Nobody asked, "Can I get you something from the bar?" I almost felt let down!

When it was time for the champagne toasts, I picked up my water glass. I felt self-conscious, but nobody seemed to be taking any notice. Then I glanced across the room and saw one man toasting the bride with a can of Pepsi. (Looking back, maybe he was recovering. Maybe he wasn't. Maybe he was a teetotaler. A Mormon. It doesn't matter.) I was starting to gain insights at that wedding. That toast was not about "looking good" — about my conforming and having a glass of champagne with everybody else — but about paying a tribute to the bride and groom. It wasn't about *me*. It was about *them*.

And it was another stage of my growing "normality"; I was beginning to recognize that there were other people in the world besides myself. This incredible *I* was not always the message. The self-centeredness was gradually slipping away.

And it's a feeling of tremendous relief.

There's a phrase in the Big Book that says, "Relieve me of the bondage of self, that I may better do Thy will.* (It's from the Third Step prayer, the one Sally and I said together in the bathroom the night we flushed her cocaine down the toilet.) Today I understand "Thy will" is to be happy and productive and enjoy the wonderment of the world. I realize that with self-centeredness in the way, I couldn't enjoy anything.

---

* From the Big Book, *Alcoholics Anonymous*, 3rd ed. (New York: A.A. World Services, Inc., 1976), 63.

So, after that wedding, the months passed. I was working my program. Slowly, I was gaining more insights. (They come when they're ready. Today, seven years into recovery, I'm still gaining insights.) In that first year, I was recovering without really knowing that I was recovering.

Then one day, about six months into sobriety, I was meeting a date for lunch at a Greek restaurant near the harbor. It was a beautiful day. Everything around me — the water, the sun-splashed buildings — seemed to be shining. I suddenly realized that perhaps for the first time in my adult life, I felt genuinely happy.

It was a new kind of joy. It's hard to explain, but I finally felt that I belonged, that I had a place in the universe. I was no longer the eternal outsider looking in. I was joining the human race.

Like Terry, I was at ease.

When I was drinking, I used to wake up every morning feeling anxious. I would lie there in bed wondering what bad things would happen that day. I had a sense of impending doom. In recovery, that fear was removed. Today, I wake up with the feeling that whatever happens can be handled.

And there has been a lot to handle. Many things have happened to me in recovery that felt difficult. Losses and challenges. I was fired from my job selling corporate art. (It was because I was so disoriented in early sobriety.) Betty, the stepmother who loved me enough to call the police, died. My younger brother Jimmy died too. Of alcoholism.

Jimmy, the chubby blonde baby who once crawled across the trailer floor while my father beat his bare legs with a hose. The little boy who was everyone's favorite. He was in his early thirties, with a wife and a baby, when he died. He had been in recovery for a year. Then Jimmy slipped.

Alcohol enlarges the veins in the throat, and sometimes they burst. He slipped once. And he died.

So many thoughts flooded my mind afterward. *But he only drank beer*, I thought. (As if I didn't know, intellectually, that

189

beer is alcohol.) *He was so young,* I thought. *It's so unfair. He should have gotten a second chance. My father is still guzzling scotch, still drinking every day, and he's nearly 80!*

It was Jimmy's death that underscored for me what a tragic disease alcoholism is. It's both predictable and unpredictable. What is predictable is that, as long as you drink, it will get worse. Bad things will happen to you. A conglomeration of bad things in anyone's life is part of the disease of alcoholism. The only elements of unpredictability are *what* those bad things will be.

* * *

Bloom where you're planted.
— Author Unknown

* * *

Epilogue

It's 7:00 P.M. and I'm alone in my third-floor office. Everyone else in the building appears to have gone home. I'm still here because I'm finishing up the last few pages of this book. File folders, holding chapters that still need revision, litter the carpet. A pile of notes rests underneath a framed photograph of my daughter Deanna's wedding.

And I'm feeling such joy at being alive.

My life today seems filled with wonderful things. My daughters Deanna and Tandice are now my closest friends. Deanna's husband, Randy, is as close as any son could be. My book is almost complete. My company is flourishing too. What a year!

Seven years ago, in the days of early sobriety, I used to huddle in my chair at my meetings, feeling absolutely worthless as a human being. I had no idea then that I would become a successful entrepreneur. I had no idea that I would enter a new profession — and own my own company.

I did know that I wanted to get back into a helping profession. I'd been a psychologist and a professor for most of my working life.

Yvonne, (my "same-length-in-sobriety" buddy) was studying for her Ph.D. in clinical psychology around that time. "Would you like me to help you?" I asked her. Yvonne said she certainly would. We began working together regularly, usually spreading all her papers out on my dining room table.

One evening, I glanced up from the table at the chandelier hanging over us. I was mesmerized by the dazzle of the light. And, suddenly, I *knew*.

"Yvonne," I said, "I'm going to be a psychologist again."

She looked up from her papers and said calmly, "Of course you are."

* * *

Why did I decide to include so much of my personal story in this book?

Well . . . it wasn't easy. (There were parts that I used to mutter over, "That's so embarrassing. Do I really want to put *that* in?") It meant trusting you with the intimate details of my life. Trusting you not to judge me.

I did it because I wanted to speak to you in a very personal way — a way in which I wish someone had spoken to me long before I found the program of recovery. I wanted to speak to you as a friend.

The reason those of us who are recovering tell our personal stories is to share our experience, strength, and hope.

The *strength* is in the program. It's in the other people who surround you. And the hope? The hope is for the future. By saying to you, "This is the truth of my life," I hope to share with you my ever-increasing sense of optimism.

I still have days when I feel down, feel blue, feel isolated, feel like fighting with someone. Days when I just want to run away and be irresponsible. There are still moments, although they're fewer and fewer, when fear and panic wrench my heart. But today, those feelings don't put me at risk. They simply remind me that I'm a human being. That I'm just like other people. I have *feelings*.

That's what sobriety has given me, one day at a time. It's a sense of simplicity. I know I'm not a Wonderwoman. (You will never find me, today, scooping out thirteen pumpkins for guests to eat soup out of.) But I don't feel I have to be Wonderwoman. Just a human woman.

Everything I need today — recovery — is available to me. And what I want today is everything! And more of it! I'm not afraid of that, of taking risks.

What do we as recovering women want? And need?

Well, if we are in very early sobriety, risk taking can probably wait for a while. In early sobriety, we need comfort. Kindness. Loving support. (The kind I got from my sponsor, Annalee.) We also need laughter. A lot of laughter.

Then, taking things slowly, easily, we need to discover who we really are. When we are no longer afraid to take the risk of being ourselves, we will realize that we no longer have to "look good," we *are* good. All of us can gain so much strength, so much encouragement from each other.

I'll leave you with a quote that seemed to me to be a perfect way of saying good-by to you. It's from the Big Book, and it implies that recovery is open ended. Forever.

> *Abandon yourself to God as you understand God. Admit your faults to Him and to your fellows. Clear away the wreckage of your past. Give freely of what you find and join us. We shall be with you in the Fellowship of the Spirit, and you will surely meet some of us as you trudge the road of Happy Destiny.*
> — ALCOHOLICS ANONYMOUS*

---

*From the Big Book, *Alcoholics Anonymous*, 3rd ed. (New York: A.A. World Services, Inc., 1976), 164.

Other titles that will interest you . . .

Each Day a New Beginning
Daily Meditations for Women
    Written by a recovering woman, this meditation book helps us find strength and direction from our Higher Power and other recovering women. 400 pp.
Order No. 1076

Some Days
Notes from the Heart of Recovery
    by the author of *Each Day a New Beginning*
    This candid look at the ups and downs of recovery offers guidance for seeking spiritual progress—not perfection—in recovery. Affirming quotations from *Each Day a New Beginning* combine with thoughtful journal entries to bring us closer to understanding how we can foster spiritual growth. 96 pp.
Order No. 5074

WomanWords
A Journal for My Self
    A blank journal created especially for women, by women, *WomanWords* taps into the positive power of being a woman. Creamy pages come alive with graceful sweeps of color and affirming messages from popular Hazelden women authors. 96 pp.
Order No. 8301

For price and order information please call one of our Telephone Representatives. Ask for a free catalog describing nearly 1,500 items available through Hazelden Educational Materials.

HAZELDEN EDUCATIONAL MATERIALS

1-800-328-9000   1-800-257-0070   1-612-257-4010   1-612-257-2195
(Toll Free. U.S. Only) (Toll Free. MN Only) (AK and Outside U.S.)   (FAX)

Pleasant Valley Road • P.O. Box 176 • Center City, MN 55012-0176